The Cycling
ANTHOLOGY

VOLUME FIVE

# The Cycling ANTHOLOGY

## VOLUME FIVE

Edited by
Ellis Bacon
&
Lionel Birnie

YELLOW JERSEY PRESS
LONDON

Published by Yellow Jersey Press 2014

2 4 6 8 10 9 7 5 3 1

Copyright © Peloton Publishing 2014

Each author has asserted their right under the Copyright, Designs
and Patents Act 1988 to be identified as the author of their work

This book is sold subject to the condition that it shall not,
by way of trade or otherwise, be lent, resold, hired out,
or otherwise circulated without the publisher's prior
consent in any form of binding or cover other than that
in which it is published and without a similar condition,
including this condition, being imposed on the subsequent purchaser

First published in Great Britain in 2014 by
Yellow Jersey Press
Random House, 20 Vauxhall Bridge Road,
London SW1V 2SA

www.vintage-books.co.uk

Addresses for companies within The Random House Group Limited can
be found at: www.randomhouse.co.uk/offices.htm

The Random House Group Limited Reg. No. 954009

A CIP catalogue record for this book
is available from the British Library

ISBN 9780224092425

The Random House Group Limited supports the Forest Stewardship
Council® (FSC®), the leading international forest-certification organisation.
Our books carrying the FSC label are printed on FSC®-certified paper.
FSC is the only forest-certification scheme supported by the
leading environmental organisations, including Greenpeace.
Our paper procurement policy can be found at:
www.randomhouse.co.uk/environment

FSC
MIX
Paper from
responsible sources
FSC® C016897
www.fsc.org

Printed in Great Britain by Clays Ltd, St Ives plc

# THE CYCLING ANTHOLOGY

7      THE NEUTRALISED ZONE
         INTRODUCTION BY THE EDITORS

9      SOLDIERS OF THE ROAD
         BRENDAN GALLAGHER
         Cycling's war heroes and the role of the
         bicycle in World War One

29      IN SEARCH OF PANACHE
         JEREMY WHITTLE
         Why you don't have to be a winner to be a winner
         in the public's eyes

45      INTO THE OPEN ERA
         FRANÇOIS THOMAZEAU
         How the Tour de France became the international
         event it is today

60      OH, TOUR!
         ELLIS BACON
         Reliving the 2014 Tour de France – in poetry

73      LINDA McCARTNEY ON TOUR
         LIONEL BIRNIE
         The story behind what could have become one of
         Britain's best-ever cycling teams

# THE CYCLING ANTHOLOGY

117     THE MYSTERY OF JOEY
        McLOUGHLIN
        ANDY McGRATH
        What ever happened to one of the biggest stars of
        '80s and '90s British cycling?

143     SUPERBAGNÈRES
        EDWARD PICKERING
        A return to one of cycling's greatest Pyrenean climbs

159     THE SOUNDS OF CYCLING
        MATT BEAUDIN
        The Tour de France is a treat for the senses – albeit
        a loud one

175     TREADING THE BOARDS
        MATT McGEEHAN
        Wish you were here – a postcard from the 2014
        track World Championships in Colombia

198     THE COGNAC SALESMAN AND
        THE CONMAN
        DANIEL FRIEBE
        Meet Jean François Naquet-Radiguet:
        Tour de France pioneer

# THE NEUTRALISED ZONE

## INTRODUCTION BY THE EDITORS

The Cycling Anthology is now into its fifth volume – a new collection of wholly original writing, as always, by some of the world's top cycling writers, whose names you'll no doubt recognise from magazines, newspapers and websites.

While our contributors come from all over the world – Europe, South America, Australia, North America – the Anthology nevertheless remains a predominantly British 'product' simply by virtue of the fact that it was conceived in Britain, and is put together, edited and printed in Britain, too.

The United Kingdom enjoyed hosting two of the three Grand Tours in 2014: first, the start of the Tour of Italy in Belfast and Armagh in Northern Ireland, followed by the Tour de France's *Grand Départ* in Yorkshire.

Both events were a phenomenal success, but British riders didn't have as charmed a season as they'd had the previous couple of years. At the Tour de France, in particular, we saw the UK's biggest names either not start or crash out of the race, and fans instead enjoyed the almost phoenix-like re-emergence of French riders. And that has been reflected in the Anthology by the inclusion of a native French-speaking writer — François Thomazeau — for the first time.

Let us hope that our net of contributors will be thrown even wider in future, and that bike racing, too, continues to seek out and discover new places, faces, fans and races.

Enjoy the read.

**Ellis Bacon & Lionel Birnie**

# 1

In 2014, the centenary of the start of the First World War forced people to remember the fallen, and reflect on the futility of war.

The First World War was also responsible for the deaths of three Tour de France winners – Lucien Petit-Breton, François Faber and Octave Lapize – while countless other champion cyclists were also to lose their lives while fighting for their countries.

**Brendan Gallagher** recounts some of their stories, and takes a closer look at the role the bicycle played during the war.

# SOLDIERS OF THE ROAD

## BRENDAN GALLAGHER

Historians broadly accept that approximately 10 million soldiers and 7 million civilians died in the First World War, while there were a further 20 million soldiers and civilians injured: appalling statistics that take no account of the estimated 20 million exhausted souls who then perished in the Spanish flu pandemic that swept the globe at the end of hostilities.

Against such a tidal wave of death and destruction, some may consider it a frivolous exercise to examine the contribution of one small sector of society – cyclists – to such a scene of devastation, and they may well be correct.

I take the view, however, that systematically looking at the smaller picture – in fact, hundreds upon hundreds of smaller pictures – offers perhaps the only real chance of glimpsing the bigger picture, which is impossible to take in at first glance.

The year 2014 has been nothing if not a monumental and sobering learning experience for those generations fortunate enough never to be touched by a world war. How blessed we are. I am sitting down to pen this early in August – on the hundredth anniversary of the outbreak of the First World War – and, even as a history graduate, I am appalled at my ignorance of that war. I have sat and passed exams on the subject, but learned next to nothing. I had no idea, until I came across a brilliant BBC2 documentary about the massive role played by African and Asian conscripts from the various empires – British, French and Belgian, in particular – who were thrown into the worst excesses of the Western Front from day one. Cannon fodder, literally.

Equally, I was ignorant of the fact that, for the majority of the war, British Forces snootily turned their backs on volunteer women nurses from these islands looking to treat our 'brave boys' behind the trenches, and that many ended up caring instead for the French, Belgian and other allied troops. They never taught us that at school. In a real sense, many of us are only truly discovering the First World War now, and in that respect you can never have too much investigation and knowledge. We can't change a damned thing, but we can remember and commemorate and that process should never stop.

Until this 'summer of learning', I still only had the vaguest idea of how many big-name cyclists were involved in the First World War. Some fought and perished – no fewer than three Tour de France winners were killed, while others 'survived', although the

quality of life they were left with was often nearly as
bad as death itself. The most robust of them were
back racing just months after the madness ended,
finding solace in the familiarity of old haunts and the
rhythms of a daily routine that did not involve death
and maiming.

I had never realised the important role of the
cycling regiments, with their couriers, scouts, messen-
gers and highly mobile combatants, especially early in
the war, before mechanisation took a grip. Flicking
through one of the many superb coffee-table publications that have heralded the centenary, I noticed a
striking picture with a pile of five bikes hastily thrown
to one side of a field in the mud, as you would before a
pick-up football match down the park on a summer's
evening, which puzzled me until my eyes tracked right
and there were five British soldiers crouched in a thick
hedgerow, their rifles aimed in the general direction
of the Germans. To my inexpert eyes, they looked
like the conventional civilian roadsters those same
youngsters might have ridden doing their butchers'
or grocers' rounds back in Britain five or six months
earlier. It was a strangely haunting image – that close
proximity between normality and insanity.

Having educated myself a little more on the subject,
I would make no particular grandiose claims for cyclists
during the First World War. Men go to war, do their bit,
behave well or not so well, and either enjoy good luck

or bad. The fact remains, however, that the military battlegrounds of Flanders and beyond were bloody arenas populated largely by males between the ages of sixteen and forty, where physical fitness, durability, courage, initiative, selfless teamwork, a facility with machinery and often sheer bloody-mindedness counted for much. And in that hell-hole, cyclists of all ages and abilities generally proved good soldiers with interesting stories to tell, a few of which we should tarry over: minuscule parts of the mosaic that make up the bigger picture.

Where to begin? I think we had better get the awkward bit out of the way first and recognise that in the very early days of the First World War, one of cycling's most-celebrated figures was something of a gung-ho warmonger, although, as ever, words and actions need to be placed in the context of time and place.

The celebrated Henri Desgrange, the editor of the sports newspaper *L'Auto*, and credited as the founder of the Tour de France in 1903 after a suggestion from his humble minion Géo Lefèvre, was a hard man on and off a bike. The former holder of twelve world records on the track, he famously insisted that the physical challenge posed by the Tour de France needed to be so severe that ideally only one rider would finish or survive.

Where did this fanaticism come from? Some attribute it to the spirit of exploration that then prevailed, pushing the body to extremes as exemplified by the

race to both Poles, and the emerging sport of moun-
taineering. Driving the body to the point of death
in some noble pursuit was to be celebrated rather
than feared. Perhaps there was an element of that
but, within French society in particular, the mania
for extreme physical fitness, the Olympian state of
body and mind sought by the International Olympic
Committee's founder, Baron de Coubertin, and the
extremism demanded by Desgrange, was more the
result of the humiliations of the Franco–Prussian war
which ended in 1871 and the urgent need to bolster
French manhood against the ever-present Germanic
threat. The French were going as soft as their cheese.

Within days of war being declared, Desgrange was
exhorting the readers of *L'Auto* – the pick of the crop
physically in France, the young bucks the nation desperately needed to fight the impending war – to take
up arms against the Germans with a glad heart. I am
indebted to Graham Healy, author of *The Shattered
Peloton,* who unearthed the following remarkable
extract from an editorial Desgrange wrote on the eve
of the Great War. To heighten its impact, the piece
was printed in red ink, although frankly little embel-
lishment was required.

My little fellas, my darling little fellas, my
darling little French fellas [Desgrange always
addressed his readers in this rather flowery

fashion]. The Prussians are bastards, I use this word not to mean 'lucky' but in the literal sense. Listen to me very carefully, you have to go and get those bastards. Believe it. It is impossible for a French man to fall in front of what is a German man. It is a big match to fight, use all your tricks. But watch out. When your rifle is on their chest they will ask for forgiveness but don't let them trick you, pull the trigger without pity. We have to get rid of these evil imbeciles. It's all down to you my little fellas, my darling little fellas, my darling little French fellas.

Extraordinary, inflammatory, racist stuff from a man of extremes in the midst of heightened times. But also the words of a clever, much-read, commercially astute editor who knew his audience of fit young sportsmen – mainly cyclists, although the paper was still giving space to other sports at this time. It should also be conceded that Desgrange, on this occasion, put his money where his mouth was. After setting up a number of fitness camps to train young military recruits, he then, at the age of fifty, enlisted in 1917 and served as a *poilu* – an ordinary soldier – in which capacity he was awarded the *Croix de Guerre*. All the time he continued to file a column for *L'Auto* under the by-line of Desgrenier.

Cycling – as a cog within the vastly complicated war machine – was already well established within various militia before the outbreak of the war. Prior to 1914, there were already fifteen cycling battalions in the 15,000-strong British Army Cyclist Corps – the Huntingdon and Highland Cycling Battalions were among the most celebrated – and they were promptly absorbed into frontline regiments and were right to the fore in the opening months of hostilities. Among those were the Norfolk, Suffolk, Essex, East Yorkshire and London Regiments, the Royal Scots, the Isle of Wight Rifles, the Hampshire Regiment, the Welsh Regiment and the Devonshire Regiment.

Additionally, nineteen new cycling battalions were quickly established, and even those regiments that didn't incorporate cycling battalions would designate soldiers to undertake cycling duties. In all, it's estimated that 100,000 British soldiers saw active service on a bike at some stage between 1914 and 1918. Among the French and Belgian armies, the figure was closer to 150,000, while the use of bikes was commonplace in German infantry battalions, which all included cycling sections, or *Radfahr-Kompanie*. Indeed, after the war, the Germans even published a report, entitled *Die Radfahrertruppe*, about the effectiveness of the bike in war.

What exactly did these cycling regiments and detachments do? An admittedly rather gushing and not unbiased article in *Cycling Weekly* in October 1914 explained it thus:

> The reasons of the success of the soldier-cyclist are not far to seek. In the first place it must be realised that his mount, unlike that of the cavalryman, is silent in progress. This gives him an enormous advantage over his noisy foe, whose horse betrays his presence even when galloping over grassland. In short, the cyclist can hear and not be heard. He can approach speedily and noiselessly, and without warning can attack the enemy, who, all unconscious of his presence, often falls an easy prey.
>
> But silence is by no means the cyclist's sole advantage. He has a good turn of speed, which is a factor useful alike in attack and retreat. A cyclist in warfare is really a mounted infantryman, and, generally speaking, he is superior in point of speed to the heavily accoutred cavalryman, while, of course, the ordinary infantryman is snail-like by comparison. Should his attack fail for the time being, or receive an unexpected or momentary check, the cyclist can easily beat a retreat, and by a circuitous route come upon his foe again at another point, where, perhaps, he is least expected. Thus he can be said to possess to a marked degree the power to 'cut

and come again' which faculty is eminently useful in war. Again, the ability to take cover often spells the difference between victory and defeat, and here the cyclist scores distinctly. He has but to lay his mount down flat upon the ground and it is practically invisible.

There were essentially three sorts of bikes used in the First World War by British troops. There was the common roadster, adapted with front carriers and clips to carry rifles, while the sturdier military roadster – constructed by either BSA, Phillips, Royal Enfield or Raleigh – would be fitted with rear and front carriers, rifle clips, machine-gun placements and other attachments so that stretchers could be slung between two or sometimes three bikes, and casualties raced to a field hospital. Finally, there was the innovative Dursley-Pedersen Detachable Military Cycle, which could be folded up and carried on your back when the terrain got too rough.

* * *

It was actually a reconnaissance cyclist, John Henry Parr – a private in the 4th Battalion of the Middlesex Regiment – who is commonly accepted as the first British military casualty of the Great War. Over 700,000 were to follow. Parr was on patrol, on his push bike, with a small detachment north of Mons in southern Belgium on 21 August 1914, trying to determine the location of German forces who were advancing much more quickly than had been anticipated. They were intercepted and attacked, and it appears Parr climbed off his bike and offered covering fire from a ditch to allow his colleagues to escape on their bikes before he was shot and killed.

Such was the confusion and chaos in the early stages of the war that the full details of Parr's death only emerged four years later. Parr's mother, Alice, back home in Finchley, had been worried by the lack of contact from her son during September and October, and contacted his regiment to ask after him.

In January 1915, his regiment still erroneously thought he was alive and serving, and wrote back to that effect, but Alice, in her heart, knew differently having received a letter from a prisoner of war saying he had seen her son shot in action near Mons in August.

The regiment double-checked, and eventually confirmed the date and rough location of his death, although it wasn't until after the war that a fellow officer, one of those who had made his escape by bike, filled in a few of the details of their patrol outside the village of Bettignies.

Young John Parr had just turned seventeen when he died, although his headstone at the nearby St Symphorien cemetery lists him as twenty. Like many

others, Parr, whose only other employment had been
as a golf caddy at North Middlesex Golf Club, had
falsified his age when he had signed up in 1913 well
ahead of hostilities. On enlisting, the barrack-room
wags immediately christened their youngest colleague
'Old Par' – a reference to Old Tom Parr, the mythical
Englishman who reputedly lived to the age of 152 and
fathered a child at the age of one hundred.

Parr's grave at St Symphorien, one of the few cem-
eteries on the Western Front that houses both Allied
and German soldiers, is situated just seven yards away
from the grave of the last British soldier to die in the
First World War: George Edwin Ellison, who was shot
by a sniper just ninety minutes before the Armistice
was signed on 11 November 1918.

Objectively, did the cyclists and their bikes fulfil
a valid military role? We should probably leave that
assessment to Sir John French, Commander-in-Chief
of the British Expeditionary Force, whose comments to the House of Lords were quoted in *The War
Illustrated* in November 1915.

> I am anxious in this despatch to bring to your
> Lordship's special notice the splendid work
> that has been done throughout the campaign
> by the Cyclists of the Signal Corps. Carrying
> despatches and messages at all hours of the
> day and night in every kind of weather, and

often traversing bad roads blocked with transport, they have been conspicuously successful in maintaining an extraordinary degree of efficiency in the service of communications. Many casualties have occurred in their ranks, but no amount of difficulty or danger has ever checked the energy and ardour which has distinguished this corps.

Their contribution certainly seemed to strike a chord with the public. To mark the contribution of British cyclists to the Great War, a memorial was unveiled on 21 May 1921 on the village green at Meriden – the only dedicated memorial to the fallen of a specific sport, rather than a specific team, in Britain that I know of. Situated in the very heart of England, contemporary reports claim that 20,000 cyclists travelled to Meriden for the unveiling ceremony and associated events that weekend.

* * *

As mentioned, three Tour de France winners lost their lives in the Great War: Octave Lapize, Lucien Petit-Breton and François Faber. When normal service was resumed in 1919, the Tour organisers ordered a three-minute silence before the start of the first stage to mark their passing. These were arguably the three biggest names in the sport, so their deaths had an impact and poignancy beyond the norm.

The demise of the dashing Lapize hit particularly hard. Lapize had unhesitatingly joined the French Air Corps the moment war was declared, training as a fighter pilot, but he was lost in the skies above Pont-à-Mousson in north-east France when attacked by two enemy aircraft. The Parisian was one of cycling's great all-rounders – a deft bike handler and an athlete of immense versatility and panache, and so it was perhaps unsurprising that he opted to join the fledgling Air Corps. Ironically, his love affair with aeroplanes began on a rest day in Caen during his successful 1910 Tour when he was treated to a flight in a Blériot piloted by celebrated aviator Léon Morane. From that moment on, Lapize was hooked.

Lapize was also a Six-Day champion on the track, and in 1907 was both the French cyclo-cross champion and the national road-race champion. He also won the Paris–Roubaix and Paris–Brussels one-day races three times each.

Known as *Le Frisé* thanks to his curly hair, Lapize is probably best remembered in the modern era as the rider who accused the Tour organisers – headed by Desgrange – of being 'assassins' during the first-ever epic mountain stage in the Pyrenees in 1910, after he had conquered the Col du Tourmalet but then struggled mightily on the Col d'Aubisque. Having vented his feelings, he descended like a madman to make good a fifteen-minute deficit on François Lafourcade – another to join the French air force and lose his life – to win the stage and, ultimately, the race that year.

Desgrange, despite his well-documented demands for courage and displays of virility from his French countrymen, was already safely installed in the first-class luxury of a train bound for Paris, having correctly sensed the imminent outrage of the peloton after they had been asked to scale the Pyrenees. It was his underlings who had to deal with the widespread displeasure among the peloton.

Today, riders who conquer the Tourmalet will find a memorial to Lapize at its summit.

A perennial rival of Lapize's was François Faber – the so-called 'Giant of Colombes' on account of his imposing six foot two, fourteen-stone physique, which made him look more like a French flanker than a champion cyclist. Faber, of dual French and Luxembourg nationality, won the 1909 Tour, which was raced in particularly bad weather, and in all won nineteen Tour stages, with the last coming in 1914 when the Tour started on the day that Archduke Franz Ferdinand of Austria was fatefully assassinated in Sarajevo.

Faber had no doubts when war was declared the following month that it was his duty to volunteer, and decided to join the French Foreign Legion in August 1914, which operated mainly at home. Not only did he look the part, but he quickly became an efficient and much admired corporal in the legion. For many years, a widely reported story persisted that he died when shot by a sniper near Arras on 9 May 1915 when jumping for joy after receiving a telegram announcing the news that his wife had just given birth to their baby daughter.

Other reports, however, state he was shot, nevertheless on the same day, while carrying a wounded colleague back from no-man's-land between Carency and Mont-Saint-Eloi. The fact that he was posthumously awarded the *Médaille Militaire* surely gives greater credence to the latter. Whatever the truth, Faber fell in a firestorm of a battle, his regiment losing 1,950 out of 2,900 personnel in their attack. Today his life is commemorated with the GP François Faber – a one-day bike race in Luxembourg – and there is a plaque in his memory in the Notre Dame de Lorette church in the French National War Cemetery near Arras.

The third great Tour hero killed in the war was the suave, Argentinian-reared Frenchman Lucien Petit-Breton – a great crowd favourite, especially with the ladies. A rather exotic individual, Petit-Breton was born in France but brought up in Buenos Aires where, after winning a bike as a lottery prize, he took to cycling with aplomb, learning to ride on the track before moving back to France where he enjoyed a first brief spell in the French army before concentrating on his cycling. Petit-Breton won the first-ever Milan–San Remo in 1907, and went on to win the Tour de France that year, and again the following year for good measure. Nothing would ever really top those glory years, although in 1911 he also added a stage win at the Tour of Italy to his *palmarès*.

At the outbreak of war, Petit-Breton joined the Army Driving Corps and was heavily involved in the famous *taxis de la Marne* episode early in the war, when every available driver and vehicle, including the Paris taxi fleet, were pressed into action to transport French troops to the First Battle of the Marne as the Germans closed in on the French capital.

Petit-Breton served extensively close to the front, but he was actually twenty miles behind the lines when he was killed on 20 December 1917, reportedly swerving in the middle of the night to avoid a horse and cart being driven erratically by its drunken owner.

The French Air Corps tended to be a popular option for adventurous members of the peloton. Albert Delrieu and Emile Quaissard were both killed in action, while Henri Alavoine – brother of the more famous Jean – joined up but was killed in a training-flight accident near Pau in 1916. Another to meet that fate was the Swiss rider Emile Guyon who also died in an accident near Pau in 1918, just a month before hostilities ceased.

On the Italian front, probably the most celebrated cyclist to see service was Ottavio Bottecchia, although at the time his prowess as a cyclist was not evident. Bottecchia, a bricklayer from Colle Umberto in the Veneto, joined the *Bersaglieri* – Italy's light-infantry corps – when war was declared and, using a bike, proved an outstanding scout and message-runner in the Veneto region, which he knew like the back of his hand. In particular, he earned praise for transporting rifles and small machine guns to the front on his bike, and for his bravery under fire. So adept and strong was he on a bike that an officer suggested he became a cyclist after the war, which is exactly what he did, winning the Tour de France in 1924 and 1925.

Bottecchia met a strange and still unexplained death in June 1927 when his battered and cut body was found on the roadside near his home after a training ride. His nearby bike was undamaged, and the generally accepted, but unproven, explanation is that he was assassinated for his outspoken anti-Fascist comments.

Elsewhere, Belgian champion Paul Deman narrowly avoided execution by the Germans for his work in the Belgian resistance when he hid messages in a specially adapted gold tooth. The declaration of peace came just in time for Deman, who clearly recovered his poise quickly, because just over a year later he enjoyed another of his finest moments, winning the

1920 Paris–Roubaix, having already won the first edition of the Tour of Flanders prior to the war in 1913.

Not every cyclist enjoyed a 'good war'. Henri Pélissier finished second in the 1917 running of the Tour of Lombardy, which was held throughout the war, but then managed to engineer an unlikely discharge from the French army soon afterwards due to his 'incredibly weak constitution'. The stricken Pélissier then recovered sufficiently to win the 1919 Paris–Roubaix, which caused a raised eyebrow or two. But in 1935 he was killed by his lover after he attacked her wielding a knife – shot dead with the same gun that Pélissier's wife had used to kill herself in 1933.

Nobody has yet been able to accurately calculate the number of casualties from the peloton during the First World War due to important records having been destroyed during World War II, but the official book of the history of the centenary Tour de France insists it is well over fifty. 145 riders lined up in Paris for the start of the 1914 Tour, while only sixty-seven started the 1919 race, which tells its own story in graphic fashion.

As Bertrand Russell famously commented, 'War does not determine who is right – only who is left.'

**Brendan Gallagher** has been a sports journalist for thirty years, serving his apprenticeship in South Wales and as a director of Hayters Sports Agency before a twenty-year stint at the coalface with the *Daily Telegraph*, proudly writing on any sport except football. He has ghosted Irish rugby union player Brian O'Driscoll's autobiography as well as *In Pursuit of Glory* and *On Tour* for Bradley Wiggins. He also wrote the official LOCOG history of Great Britain and the Olympics ahead of the 2012 Games. In a lighter vein, he indulged his love of comic-book heroes by compiling biographical histories of Wilson of the Wizard, Alf Tupper – the Tough of the Track, and Roy of the Rovers in *Sporting Supermen*.

Brendan is currently working for *The Rugby Paper*, the Tour of Britain website and is completing a history of the rugby World Cup.

# 2

Panache. Who's got it? Who hasn't got it? And who wishes they did have it? When you're not a proven, calculating, clockwork winner, you require something else to thrill the fans.

Professional bike riders either have to win or prove that they can help a teammate win in order to get their next contract. Doomed efforts in breakaways, dangling in front of a hungry peloton, are worth little unless the TV cameras take a liking to you. And for that to happen, you have to do, say or be something a little special.

When it comes to panache, **Jeremy Whittle** discovers, you've either got it or you ain't.

# IN SEARCH OF PANACHE

## JEREMY WHITTLE

The Massif Central, July 2005.

I'm loitering, a little aimlessly, in the meadow serving as the *parking équipes* at the side of Mende's old aerodrome, sometimes a finish line to stages in Paris–Nice and, on this hot summer afternoon, to the eighteenth stage of the Tour de France.

I have panache on my mind. As Lance Armstrong closes on the seventh of his 'deadly sins', he is being accused of many things – cheating, bullying, fraud, deceit, relentless control-freakery – and a lack of panache.

Across the paddock, Johan Bruyneel gets out of his team car, stands up, and stretches his back. He rummages through the detritus of a long hot day in the Massif Central, fiddling with road books, empty coffee cups and radios. This is also something *directeurs sportifs* do when they see journalists approaching and want to create a pretence of being busy performing essential tasks.

I wait until Johan has finished his fiddling.

'Johan,' I begin, 'a lot of French journalists are saying that this victory lacks panache because Lance hasn't yet won a stage in this Tour…'

Bruyneel looks taken aback, then slightly amused.
'Really. They are…?' he says.

There's a brief pause, then a triumphant smirk begins playing on his lips as he realises he is developing the perfect rebuke.

'Well,' he continues, puffing out his chest a little, '*I* think winning seven Tours gives you panache.'

There's a snort and a guffaw from some of those now gathered around us.

'What a smart-arse,' I think, before stomping off, but then I never liked Bruyneel.

\* \* \*

'All this panache business – they can kiss my arse, these people,' says the wife of Britain's first-ever Tour de France winner. 'Who's got panache? These people that go on stupid, pointless attacks?'

Cath Wiggins was sounding off after her husband won the 2012 Tour de France, only to be criticised, like Armstrong, for a lack of panache. Sir Bradley might have justifiably pointed to his time-trialling prowess, his hair or his stunning wardrobe of new suits as evidence of panache. For the real romantics, however, even being top dog in the 'race of truth' doesn't seem to count.

For his part, David Millar, another man with a keen interest in style and image, describes panache as 'the last bastion of daring'.

Millar, himself the author of several moments of panache (or 'stupid, pointless attacks') – his doomed solo escape into Barcelona during the 2009 Tour being one of the most renowned – says that 'there's something a little self-destructive about panache'.

'It's throwing caution to the wind, and requires emotional rather than rational decisions. That's why it's possible to have panache in victory or defeat. You have to be indifferent to the outcome.'

Millar is among those who bemoans the predictability that now too often characterises professional racing, particularly in stage races.

'Everything is so controlled nowadays,' Millar says. 'It's easy to forget the sport was founded on panache, a "he who dares, wins" attitude,' although he adds: 'We took that a bit too far for a long time…'

But was cycling *really* founded on panache? Has panache really ever stood for a tangible quality, a noble athletic characteristic, beyond some sepia-tinted memory of the good old days, when climbers took eighteen minutes in the Chartreuse or a quarter of an hour on the steep hairpins of the Mercantour massif?

And how closely – as Millar himself accepts – was that ideal of a cycling exploit intertwined with doping? After all, Bjarne Riis at Hautacam, Lance Armstrong on Alpe d'Huez, Marco Pantani at Courchevel and all the others – all of those infamous performances were, for a while, subject to empty cries of '*Quel panache!*'

Now when we do witness a performance that some perhaps all-too-easily imbue with panache, we hesitate. We think of those three names – Riis, Armstrong, Pantani – then of some others, now long gone, captured supping wine, kissing the girls, or standing on a finish line in woollen jerseys, goggles, raincoats. And then we think of Vino – good old Vino.

\* \* \*

It's ironic that Vincenzo Nibali, the rider credited with bringing panache back to the Tour de France in 2014, is managed by a specialist in faking it. That's because Alexandre Vinokourov, the Sicilian's team boss, as a rider specialised in 'faux' panache – that's the kind you buy from an Italian doctor.

Real panache, personified by Hugo Koblet, Charly Gaul, Louison Bobet, Jacques Anquetil, Luis Ocaña, Laurent Fignon and second-generation Bernard Hinault has been in short supply at the Tour for several years now. Plus you also have that other little problem, of second-guessing whether the bravura performance you're watching is real.

Vino was one of the peloton's dopers and dupers – an actor playing the part of the courageous have-a-go-hero, fighting on against all odds.

Yes, yes, we all know Vino wasn't alone, that there were plenty of other fakes on the scene at that time, but there was something about Vino's schtick – the grimacing, dour, never-say-die, *I'm just a guy from the former Eastern Bloc doin' what a guy from the former Eastern Bloc's gotta do to earn a livin' around here* act – that really stuck in the throat.

In fact, I'll go further. I'll say this: Vino definitively killed panache and then tramped the dirt down. He killed it in 2007, when the Tour caravan had spat out Michael Rasmussen and, as it trundled on, hoping for signs of life – of all the old virtues of honour, sacrifice and suffering – foolishly clung to Vino, whose courage in adversity, it turned out, came from a batch of blood bags he'd made earlier.

Vino may, it is now claimed, have killed it again in 2010, when he allegedly paid off Alexandr Kolobnev to ensure he won Belgian Classic Liège–Bastogne–Liège (a case for which the result is still pending following an investigation by cycling's governing body, the UCI). And then he did it again in July 2014, when he wore an Astana-blue boxer-boy cap, reverse style, during the Tour de France. Time may judge that as his greatest crime of all.

Perhaps that moment, late July 2007 – years before the USADA report became a reality – was when most gave up on the Tour and the old ideals, one of which was the notion of panache, that a rider could achieve a state of grace even without winning, by promenading his athletic prowess, his style, his racing form.

What's more, old-fashioned panache – of the post-war kind, once served up by Hugo Koblet, Charly Gaul and Louison Bobet – now has many obstacles. The post-Festina, post-Puerto, post-Armstrong obsession with clean sport is just one of them.

The growth of corporate funded 'professionalism' within cycling, the proliferation of points systems, the search for marginal gains, the biological passport and an infatuation with sports science have all encouraged project management, return on investment and, ultimately, low-risk and sometimes tedious racing.

The 2014 Liège–Bastogne–Liège, one of the most boring Classics for many years, was even decried by its own organiser, Christian Prudhomme, after the growing obsession with racking up points for the team classification saw the race stagnate.

'It's incredibly disappointing for the hundredth edition of such a great race,' Prudhomme said afterwards. 'The real drama was played out in much too short a period – in ten kilometres out of 263. That's not very inspiring.'

The blame for a snooze-inducing 'doyen' was placed by some on the structure of the UCI World Tour and a growing reluctance to take on the risks inherent in attacking racing.

'It's because of the points classification,' Marc

Madiot, manager of the French FDJ team, said. 'If I
want my team to be in the first division next year, I
need points. I understand if spectators don't find that
very exciting but I don't have any choice.'

Of course, that's one palatable excuse for the reluctance of some to race, although there's another darker
rationale, which should encourage rather than depress
those who were sickened by the likes of Riis, Vino,
Armstrong, et al in the past.

That other rationale is that cycling is getting cleaner.
The ramping-up of anti-doping has had a significant
impact on the willingness of riders to take on mammoth breakaways, long-distance attacks, or do-or-die
moves. When in the past, in a race as brutal and long
as Liège, for example, they would have adopted a more
daring approach, knowing that 'the programme' might
see them through, instead they now have to manage
their strength.

The consensus of opinion after this year's Liège–
Bastogne–Liège supports that.

'When the race is hard, you have to wait for the last
moment,' Valerio Piva, *directeur sportif* at BMC, said.

'The general level of the teams and riders themselves is higher,' Piva's colleague, Allan Peiper, added,
while, according to Prudhomme, 'The ability of the
peloton is more and more homogenous.'

So, the days of heavyweight sparring on the Ventoux,
La Redoute, the Mortirolo or Alpe d'Huez may have

gone – if not permanently, at least for a while. Nibali's carefully considered moves in the mountain stages of the 2014 Tour hinted at a more measured attacking style.

All of which, even if you can still hope that it isn't the case, sounds ominously like another death-knell for panache. Collectively those elements have effectively killed off high-risk exploits. Now, we're forced to endure a kind of whiney and petulant imitation of panache, which brings us neatly to Thomas Voeckler.

\* \* \*

Some people will tell you that the gurning, froth-ing, special effect that is French professional Tommy Voeckler possesses panache, and that his do-or-die efforts make him a 'great' and 'stylish' rider. This assessment is based on the perennial moment in the Tour de France when his 'heroic' breakaway bid fails.

These people are wrong. The truth is that Voeckler is an empty vessel, a sham. He knows that 99 per cent of the time he will fail, but that his reputation for a music-hall version of panache is based on his overly theatrical image. He is the embodiment of what Dave Brailsford would call a 'plucky loser'.

Just ask Mick Rogers, who delighted in putting Voeckler in his place when he won in the Pyrenees in July this year.

Voeckler has developed an inbuilt 'cam-dar', so attuned to the presence of a TV camera at his side that he will respond either by 1) attacking on a descent, which always looks cool and brave, but has the added attraction of being sure to fail, or by 2) winking conspiratorially at the folks back home as he attacks 'stupidly and pointlessly', by 3) remonstrating with his breakaway companions for their lack of effort – see above reference to Mick Rogers – or by 4) puffing out his cheeks and throwing the bike from side to side as he is dropped in crosswinds on a false flat, in a bid to demonstrate just how hard he is working, usually as the peloton becomes a speck in the distance.

Maybe I'm being a little unfair: after all, we'd miss him if he wasn't there.

One of the best of many roadside YouTube clips from the 2014 Tour is of Voeckler climbing wearily and alone, far behind the bunch, to the ski station at Chamrousse. As he rounds a bend, an indeterminate babble of fans jeer beerily at him.

Outraged, he screeches – as much as you can at eight miles an hour – to a halt, in front of the camera, of course, and starts shouting back.

'Come 'ere…! You ever ridden a bike…!?'

The stunned fans apologise – 'Sorry! Sorry!' – and, after a disgruntled *fingsaintwhattheyusedtobe* head shake, Tommy pedals on.

* * *

The definition of panache has always been confusing. It is, it seems, very much in the eye of the beholder. It can be found in a lone breakaway across the pavé of the Arenberg or on the steep grades of La Redoute, framed by the final hairpins of the Stelvio or silhouetted against the bleached rocks of a windswept Mont Ventoux.

For others, it has nothing to do with winning or losing. It could be found in Andrew Talansky's gritty final ride in this year's Tour, when the American was counselled through the pain of several crashes by sports director Robbie Hunter to finish stage 11 in tears. Afterwards, as he quit the race, Talansky said he did it to honour his team and the hard work of his teammates.

So you don't always have to win to show panache. You just have to be daring, stylish, ideally alone and riding in a way that suggests some vague half-remembered ideal of romantic sporting heroism. That perhaps is why marginal gains in time trials don't really count.

That then might lead you to conclude that Jacques Anquetil, winner of five Tours de France, was, to be blunt, a bit of a dullard. But that would be far from the whole picture.

Anquetil was a conservative and calculating rider and, well, sometimes just a little boring on the bike.

Like Wiggins, he focused on playing to his strengths. Anquetil's panache came off the bike: in bars, restaurants, casinos and in the bedroom, where his complex love life became legendary.

But there was one risk-laden moment in Anquetil's racing career that will always be perceived, perhaps more than any other, as the very embodiment of panache. Frustrated by the great affection for his rival, Raymond Poulidor, in 1965, Anquetil and his manager, Raphael Geminiani, concocted a plan to win both the Dauphiné–Libéré and the 557-kilometre Classic, Bordeaux–Paris, within twenty-four hours.

After his winner's press conference at the Dauphiné, Anquetil flew by private jet from Nîmes to Bordeaux, freshened up, had a massage and ate dinner. Then, only nine hours after winning the Dauphiné, he lined up for the start of the marathon race from the Atlantic coast to the Parc des Princes.

Anquetil and the others set off at midnight. At times he was so tired that he almost nodded off, and Geminiani – famed for his ribald language – resorted to insults as a motivational tool, even pulling alongside in the team car to question his rider's sexuality. Motor-paced for the final stages, Anquetil held off Tom Simpson to claim a famous victory. Nothing like it has been achieved in the modern era.

Certainly, 'Chrono Jacques' was blessed with far greater panache than Mario Cipollini, whose

endless attempts at 'look-at-me' panache only served
to emphasise how low-rent he was. Cipollini's version of panache had little to do with racing and was
based on several simple steps: 1) talk about sex; 2)
wear some outrageous kit and talk about sex; 3) if all
else fails, take off your outrageous kit and talk about,
or better still, have, sex. For most purists, wedded to
the Bobet–Anquetil–Fignon ideal of panache, Cipo's
antics qualify as a resounding fail.

In France, Laurent Fignon was the last of the latter-
day saints of panache, a rider so concerned about his
image that he lost the 1989 Tour de France because he
wore his hair in a ponytail. There hasn't been a French
rider with such panache – that cocktail of arrogance,
insularity, attitude and rage – since Fignon.

Fignon was French cycling's Eric Cantona, always
ready with a sulk, an insult or an existential epithet,
although there were times in his blighted career that
the seagulls chose not to follow the trawler.

Only when Fignon died did those in France who'd
always decried his bad temper – Fignon won the
*Prix Citron* for grumpiest rider during the 1989 Tour
and famously said of his *coéquipiers*, 'They're paid
to be my teammates, not my friends' – realise what
they'd lost.

Bernard Hinault, Jean-Marie Leblanc, Marc Madiot
and many others all spoke of a rider with panache,
who 'feared nothing and nobody'. Fignon's *franc-parler*

– his plain-speaking, or rudeness – also made him a great TV pundit. When some young French hope put in one of Cath Wiggins's 'stupid, pointless attacks', Fignon wouldn't shrink from saying so.

'That's a great attack, Laurent! Can he stay away?' his co-commentators would gush, desperate for some hint of French success.

'Ah non, *non*!' Fignon would groan in world-weary dismay. 'That's just stupid.'

* * *

Panache always requires stylishness married to a kind of madness, or at least a display of competitive rage, that says, 'The hell with this tedious tactical stalemate – I'll show them…'

This is why the fragile Marco Pantani, despite everything else that can be said of him, did have panache, whereas Chris Froome, who calculates and is conservative, and worse, holds the handlebars as if he's firing up a jackhammer at the side of the road underneath the Hammersmith flyover, doesn't.

In the sixteen summers since Pantani was their last Tour winner, Italians have been crying out for a new and credible champion. There have been a series of false idols – from Basso to Ricco, via Savoldelli and Scarponi.

Nibali became the pragmatic solution to those disappointments, fulfilling the romantic need for a stylish

Tour winner, but failing to fuel the kind of romance and fanaticism that Pantani inspired. Instead, he was a muted hero, and one that came with caveats.

'I've always liked to attack,' he said on his way to his Tour victory, going on to suggest that 'instinct is important' and even quoting Leonardo da Vinci.

'Theory is not enough,' Nibali said. 'You also need to have heart and show courage.'

This kind of thing was of course lapped up by a French media that, after only two years, had already grown weary of Team Sky's calculating stranglehold on the peloton and the constant talk of marginal gains. This emotive talk of heart and soul, too, enabled Nibali to sidestep some more awkward questions about where all his power was coming from.

Yet of all Nibali's attacks at the 2014 Tour, the most unpredictable, the one with perhaps the greatest élan, came in the most unromantic setting – on a Sheffield ring road. We all expected him to attack at La Planche des Belles Filles, Chamrousse and Hautacam – but holding off a pursuing peloton in suburban Sheffield? Wasn't that panache?

\* \* \*

Hang on, Tommy has just stopped by my keyboard.

'Come 'ere…! Have you ever ridden a bike…!?' he bellows, albeit from a safe distance.

'Oh, err – sorry, Tommy, sorry,' I say. 'It's just that the way you ride… You're so… annoying.'

Voeckler mutters a 'Yeah? Well, what would you know…?' then shakes his head and rides off.

And that's the difference you see. Bernard Hinault wouldn't have done that. He'd have sworn, waded in, ignored the consequences. He'd have shown utter conviction and followed through. He'd have smashed the laptop and broken my nose.

Hugo Koblet, on the other hand, would have demanded satisfaction. He'd have slapped me elegantly with a driving glove, called me a cad, before glancing in the mirror, checking his hair and adjusting his cravat as he strode off.

And Maître Jacques? He'd have snorted in derision, questioned my masculinity and then asked if we had any more champagne or oysters, before chatting up my wife or daughter.

No, that's wrong – in fact, Jacques would have chatted up both. Now that's what I call panache.

---

**Jeremy Whittle**, who writes for *The Times* and was also a founding editor of *Procycling* magazine, has been covering cycling since 1993, including twenty-one Tours de France. His book, *Bad Blood,* and his collaboration with David Millar, *Racing Through the Dark*, were both shortlisted for the William Hill Sports Book of the Year award.

# 3

When **François Thomazeau** first covered the Tour de France, Bernard Hinault was the defending champion and the host nation had enjoyed a run of nine victories in eleven years.

France has endured almost thirty years of hurt since then, although the blame for that cannot be directed at François.

However, the French fall from grace has coincided with the Tour becoming an international event. As riders from the United States, Australia, Eastern Europe and Great Britain arrived, so French influence faded.

Here he charts a country's struggle to adapt and looks at the way greater diversity has changed the Tour.

# INTO THE OPEN ERA

## FRANÇOIS THOMAZEAU

Some say the 1986 Tour de France was among the most exciting of the modern era, and Richard Moore's book *Slaying the Badger*, which was turned into a fascinating documentary, goes a long way to prove it. Personally, I would pick 1989 instead for the incredible battle between Laurent Fignon and Greg LeMond and the nail-biting climax on the Champs-Élysées, or 1998 for the fascinating spectacle of a world collapsing within three weeks. Yet 1986 was definitely a very good year as I found myself thrown unexpectedly into the wild world of the Tour for the very first time. As a young trainee journalist for Reuters, it was decided I should grab my rucksack and head for Bagnères-de-Luchon out of the blue as our rivals Agence France Presse were on strike – typically – and there was a fair chance of stealing credits from the opposition, who had half a dozen men on the race at the time when Reuters used only one free-lance stringer, while American agency AP were simply shunning the race, unaware that the Tour was soon to become a major event in the United States.

It was a romantic time, when you could embark on the world's greatest travelling sporting circus without an accreditation, a car or any hotels booked in advance. I cannot remember how I made it to the foot of the Pyrenees but I soon found myself in the back of a car taking three of the few British journalists on the race around France – the legendary Mike Price, dubbed Mike the Bike, at the wheel, *Cycling Weekly*'s Keith Bingham by his side, while I stole some of the *Guardian*'s Steve Bierley's living space at the back. The presence in the peloton of Sean Kelly and Stephen Roche meant we sometimes overtook the Irish car driven by David Walsh. Phil Liggett and Paul Sherwen, John Wilcockson and the *Herald Tribune*'s Samuel Abt were the only other English speakers I can remember. In any case, English was still a very foreign language on *La Grande Boucle* and I quickly won over my politely reluctant colleagues when it came to asking for directions or choosing the wine.

Memory tends to turn the past into a better place than it was but were those really the good old days? Hardly. It has become commonplace for Tour veterans to sigh at the time when press officers and buses were inconceivable yet it did not make life easier for the would-be Tour reporter. My baptism of fire was an ominous one. Rushing out of the press room after watching the last kilometres of the stage on television, I found myself face to face with Bernard Hinault, the yellow jersey on his back, trying to get away from the media as he had just gambled and lost to LeMond on a dramatic stage to Superbagnères. I did what I still do today on a finish line: I ran behind the man shouting his name. He looked back in anger and pushed me out of the way as I was reaching him. A seasoned colleague smiled at me and said: 'This is not the way to do it.' What is the way to do it, I still don't know to this day.

A lot has changed in thirty years but the availability of riders not so much. They were certainly more approachable at the time, before the introduction of team buses and cordons, and you could find them sipping coffee at the local bar or putting on their socks in the back of the team car. But would they talk to you or the public? Cycling at the time was even more of a closed circle than it is now. Ask LeMond or the American and Australian riders who tried to be part of it then. It took time and credentials to be accepted and riders did not see it as interesting or useful to talk to the press. What for? Salaries were low, popularity depended on what you did on the bike rather than what you said. *L'Équipe* and French and Belgian television stations were the only media that mattered. One day, France's Charly Mottet started an answer to a question I was asking him by saying: 'The year I won Paris–Roubaix…'

– But Charly, you never won Paris–Roubaix.

– That's right. I was just checking you knew what you were talking about.

Cycling was still deeply rooted in a folklore of strong characters and men of few words. One of my Irish colleagues used to interview one of his national heroes by asking, 'Would you say that…' and print the question as the answer.

The 1986 Tour was probably the year when it all started to change. An English speaker, LeMond, won the Tour for the first time. And another one, Stephen Roche, would do so the year after. Controversial French tycoon Bernard Tapie had started pouring money into the sport, foreseeing its international potential, a gamble Motorola and Team Sky would later endorse. As a young journalist, I discovered I could talk about The Clash and punk rock with Ronan Pensec, who had shaved the back of his hair in the shape of the chequered jersey of his Peugeot team. While respectful of the past, riders like Jeff Bernard or Marc Madiot would join you for a beer at the bar after stages and started speaking a different language. Andy Hampsten was something else entirely, the product of a cycling culture totally alien to Belgian Classics and dodgy *soigneur* recipes. EPO probably ruined the shift in mentalities that was taking placed at the time, temporarily stopping cycling's push towards modernity.

Soon the PDM poisoning fluke would ring as an alarm, Pedro Delgado would become the first of a long list of Spanish riders to raise doubts or eyebrows, Miguel Indurain would combine sheer talent, old tricks and new techniques to dominate cycling while EPO would make l'Alpe d'Huez as flat as a Dutch tulip field. There was already a time in the late 1950s and early 1960s when cold-blooded doctors and undercover charlatans caused serious concern and turned professional cycling into an underworld of crooks and dealers. EPO certainly helped these characters so closely linked to the sport's tradition back to the forefront and they soon reclaimed control when the likes of LeMond or Hampsten had seemed to bring a little bit of fresh air.

Ironically, my nearly thirty years on the Tour de France coincided with the longest barren period for French cycling with no Tour victory since Hinault's last in 1985. While the decline of local talent after 1998 can easily be explained by the Festina scandal, the intermediate period was an interesting one as well. First of all, it was not easy to replace a rider of Hinault's stature. Let's face it, the Belgians have yet to replace Eddy Merckx and they probably never will.

The globalisation symbolised by LeMond or even Stephen Roche was certainly to blame. France, Belgium and Italy are the founding nations of the sport, much more so than Spain, who had only won the Tour once before 1988 and started to emerge as a major cycling – and sporting – force in the 1990s. And they were the countries that struggled the most to maintain a high level of performance in the past three decades. More than the rise of new nations, the phenomenon in the late 1980s and early 1990s was the emergence of new cycling 'schools', for lack of a better word, some surviving to this day. France had actually shown the way with Cyrille Guimard, who helped both Hinault and Fignon to win the Tour by introducing modern techniques of training, a bit of dietetics, a strong emphasis on improving equipment and brilliant tactical skills. Hinault, Fignon, Madiot, Mottet and Jean-René Bernaudeau were all Guimard offspring and the influence of the Guimard school of thought lives on today through teams FDJ.fr and Europcar, both managed by former Guimard riders. Spain, besides the well-loved Kelme and Euskaltel-Euskadi outfits, saw two much more important teams emerge – Reynolds, led by the highly influential former sprinter José Miguel Echavarri, and ONCE, led by university teacher Manolo Saiz. Echavarri first won the Tour with Delgado, then manufactured Miguel Indurain into an awesome riding machine before launching countless cycling talents, from Abraham Olano to Alejandro Valverde under the banners of Banesto, Caisse d'Epargne or Movistar. Echavarri's strong political support, the man's intelligence and his far-reaching network account for the team's longevity as it has now been around for thirty-five years with relatively few problems on the doping front compared to the allegations surrounding it. Echavarri's importance on what cycling became in the 1980s and 1990s is often overlooked as the man, who became a bar owner after his short-lived pro career, had the qualities attached to that trade: inside knowledge, strong friendships and discretion.

While the Saiz system gradually collapsed after the withdrawal of ONCE and the Operacion Puerto doping scandal in 2006, it survived through Johan Bruyneel, who spent much of his riding career with ONCE and took his mentor's methods to the US Postal Service team in 1999. German cycling had only had isolated stars in the past like Rudi Altig or Dietrich Thurau, but the destruction of the Berlin Wall helped it rebuild from scratch around riders from the former East Germany, such as Jan Ullrich, Olaf Ludwig, Erik Zabel or Andreas Klöden, and launch the super-strong Telekom team. At the same time, Italy was witnessing the rise not of a generation of riders but of a generation of doctors who would soon make headlines for the wrong reasons. Add EPO to the equation and you understand what a Pandora's box Tapie opened when he started investing loads of money into cycling.

In this context, it was difficult for new French talent to really emerge. Hinault's departure to Tapie's La Vie Claire squad in 1984 seriously harmed Guimard, who never quite recovered from the shock. And while strong French riders still shone in the peloton, starting with Fignon, they were all scattered around several teams: ONCE for Laurent Jalabert, Banesto

for Jeff Bernard, RMO for Mottet, even Telekom for
Madiot towards the end of his career, while Guimard
kept Fignon and hired the promising Luc Leblanc
before he moved to Festina.

From 1994, Festina was France's attempt to build
a squad capable of challenging the strong nationally
based teams appearing at the time – Banesto, ONCE,
Telekom, Motorola and Rabobank.

It was an odd period for cycling in general and for
French cycling particularly. You could tell there was
something wrong. In 1990, after clinching his first
Tour stage in Revel, Charly Mottet told the press he
had given up on the idea of one day being a contender
for the general classification. He was still fourth the
next year and finished in the top ten three times but
there was definitely a feeling that it was not worth
trying. And this from a man who finished second in
the Giro d'Italia, won three editions of the Dauphiné
Libéré and two major Classics. Charly would probably
object if I said he was one of the last clean riders of his
generation but I sincerely believe that was the problem.

Jeff Bernard had come very close to winning the
Tour in 1987 when he finished third after a spectacular
time trial victory at the top of the Ventoux, probably
one of the most extraordinary cycling efforts I've had
the chance to witness. Yet he joined Banesto in 1991
to live forever in the shadow of Indurain. A waste?
Probably, even though the man himself, though one of

the biggest mouths in cycling, would never admit it. As for Marc Madiot, he joined Germany's Team Telekom in 1992 but only lasted a year before he called it quits.

When Bruno Roussel took over Festina in 1994, he made sure to only hire riders who understood the new rules of the game. While Mottet, Bernard and Madiot still belonged to the old school when corticoids were the dominant drug and hardly altered the accepted hierarchy, Richard Virenque, Christophe Moreau and Laurent Brochard, regardless of their potential, were ready to accept what it took to be a Tour contender in the mid-1990s. Everyone knew exactly what was happening and you did not need dope tests to tell the real men from the EPO boys. Bjarne Riis, Zenon Jaskula, Evgeni Berzin, Bo Hamburger and Dario Frigo, among many others, had few admirers in the peloton. Even the French public never seriously believed that Virenque had a serious chance of winning the Tour. Yet they loved him because of his authentic climbing abilities, his apparent naivety and possibly because of his obvious flaws, which made him more human than a true champion like Anquetil or Hinault. Jalabert, who finally confessed his drug habits in 2013, also took advantage of the same partiality to losers which is part of the French spirit.

The end of the Eastern bloc played a role, too. After 1989 and Dimitri Konyshev's silver medal at the world championships in Chambéry behind LeMond, former Soviet riders appeared in almost every team and quickly identified road cycling as a 'soft sport', one so rooted in tradition and locked within limited borders that it was easy to conquer and make profit from. British Cycling later came to the same conclusions, hopefully with a less cynical approach. But EPO probably made it even easier to join the show in the early 1990s. Former Tour de France director Jean-Marie Leblanc, who sent an open letter to denounce the dangers of EPO in 1996, once confessed to me that in his mind the arrival of Eastern riders into the peloton had marked the beginning of the end of cycling as he knew and loved it.

Ironically, as the Tour grew bigger and more global, it also became even more locked into its own limitations and evils. There was no *Village Départ* at the Tour in 1986. And it was probably a brilliant idea to launch this showcase for sponsors and to turn it into a meeting point for riders, journalists and the varied population of the Tour a couple of years later. Yet the *Village Départ* isolated the Tour from the villages themselves, pushing spectators and fans behind barriers, watching the closed little world of the cycling caravan from a distance. It was not entirely wrong to describe the world of cycling at the time as a *milieu*, the French word for the underworld of organised crime. You either belonged or you did not to this club obeying their own rules and customs. And riders as well as *suiveurs* certainly believed they were above the law, part of a giant circus whose primary goal was to bring happiness and excitement into the deepest parts of France, regardless of the methods. Unfortunately, history proved that the magic circus had entirely lost its sporting credibility, a fact that most journalists of the time acknowledged without being able to prove anything. My French colleagues had to be content with using the adjective *stupéfiant* to describe the performances of Bjarne Riis, a word with the double meaning of 'stupefying' and 'drug'. The Festina scandal was hardly a surprise even though it was a sudden and welcome irruption of the real world so far kept behind the barriers inside the walls of the club – a real world with *gendarmes*, policemen and judges. As the late Pierre-Henri Menthéour put it: 'It was cataclysmic. We, the gods, were treated as criminals!'

As we know now, Festina did not change anything. It only destroyed French cycling for a quarter of a century and further opened the way to the globalisation of cycling.

After Festina, Italian cycling was also rocked by police raids at the Giro and the Operacion Puerto case confirmed that Spain was a haven for dopers. Yet doping was and remains a strictly national concern. The dopers are always foreign. Germany only turned its back on the sport once German riders confessed. Denmark was only shocked by Riis's belated admission of drug taking. Holland only cared about revelations at Rabobank. While doping was hurting the popularity of the sport in its traditional strong-holds, cycling continued to grow, conquering new territories like America, Australia or Britain, still then unaffected by the doping delusion. It is difficult to tell whether it was a conscious move by the UCI to develop their sport worldwide to counter the dev-astating effects of doping in Europe or a coincidence. Yet it was spectacular.

By the turn of the century, English had become the dominant language in the caravan. And along came Lance!

Looking back, the main contribution of Armstrong to his sport – along with the worldwide impact he undoubtedly made – was the team bus. All the other aspects – would we call them marginal gains today? – of his fantastic yet fictitious seven-year reign over the Tour were strictly traditional. His mentor Johan Bruyneel was a pure product of the Belgian old school while he had learnt all the other tricks of the trade as a rider with Manolo Saiz's infamous ONCE team. Armstrong's genius was to include in the package the faithful servants he had formed at Motorola and the advice of Italian medical guru Michele Ferrari – a bit of the best in every cycling school from the previous era. Yet the only new thing about Bruyneel was that he spoke English. That and the team bus…

Practical they are, buses. And impressive as well. One wonders how cycling survived for nearly a century

without them. But they were ultimately another way
to isolate the riders even more within the already isolated Tour enclosure. By finding shelter inside their
buses, riders not only cut off all ties with the public,
they also parted from the rest of the Tour population.
Buses were also, as we now know, a perfect way to
keep indulging in old habits away from the public eye.
They were much more than a means of transportation:
they were the materialisation of cycling's very spirit of
exclusion.

Odd to discover as I write these lines that my
nearly thirty years on the Tour are ultimately the story
of a sport largely opening to the world only to close
itself down even more than ever in the process.

Team Sky or Garmin-Sharp's decisions to let
journalists and neutral observers inside their buses
hopefully reflect a shift in mentality. Yet there are
very serious plans by Tour organisers ASO to impose
a mixed zone at the start and finish like in most stadium sports and to restrict access to the buses and the
team parking space now referred to as 'the paddock'
to rights-holding television networks. This would be
disastrous.

There is hope about the future though. Back in
1986, riders were carrying their own mental bus
around inside their heads, and I will never forget
the disarmingly sincere look in the eyes of the cheat-
ers overtly lying to me in the golden days of EPO.

However hypocritical it often was, the recent wave of confessions in the wake of the Armstrong scandal seems to have somehow brought down the barriers.

Locked inside the gilded jail of their buses, today's riders also found a way to break out of it thanks to their mobile phones. And let's face it, I never had that many cyclist pals in the past, even if most of them today are Twitter friends… Cycling is an open sport. It should remain that way. And their accessibility is for the riders both the token of their popularity as it is of their integrity. One thing the riders of 1986 probably had much more than their present counterparts was humility. And it probably came from being so close to their fans. It is probably one of the ways for the sport to move ahead in its rehabilitation programme.

---

**François Thomazeau** has covered twenty-four Tours de France since his 1986 debut for Reuters, eleven winter or summer Olympic Games and is the head of the press commission at the French Open tennis tournament. He left Reuters in 2005 to become a freelance writer for newspapers *Le Monde* and *France Soir* as well as providing a yearly tourist guide for Tour de France organisers ASO. A self-confessed anglophile, he is the author of some forty books on a wide range of subjects, including crime novels, guides to Parisian bistros, the history of his hometown of Marseille and Mod subculture.

# 4

Vincenzo Nibali's victory at the 2014 Tour de France won't go down in history as the greatest or hardest-fought-for win simply due to the premature exits of favourites Chris Froome and Alberto Contador.

But there were nevertheless plenty of exciting, emotional moments to keep the fans at the roadside, and watching at home on television, happy.

Here, **Ellis Bacon** translates some of those moments into verse for an alternative telling of the 101st Tour. Poetry in motion. Motion in poetry.

# OH, TOUR!

## ELLIS BACON

### PROLOGUE

In fair Yorkshire,
Where our scene begins,
'Neath sunny skies,
Towns bathed in grins,
Two hundred men
Line up their wheels,
Off on their way
To shouts
And squeals.
Leeds, Harrogate,
York, Sheffield
Steel
Yourselves against
What now is real:
Three weeks ahead,
Three weeks to fear.
Remember well
This start,
Yorkshire.

## I. THE SON

With royal wave,
The *Grand Départ* –
To Harrogate,
We make our start.
To the brawling, mauling
Of a flying finish,
Up for grabs,
Though the British wish
That one in particular,
Who has his eye
On victory –
A cherished prize –
Can make it his,
Can make a play,
But he is not to be the son of Harrogate
Today.

There clattered down
By his own hand,
Intakes of breath
Across the land.
Amidst the crowd,
A mother weeps.
The sun doth sink,
And the son sleeps.

And the day is done.

Up with the sun,
But the son's undone;
His path is ended here.
But let the race march on:
*Marchons, marchons!*
There's much on the menu: fear
Blubberhouses,
Greetland,
Moss,
Midhopestones,
Oughtibridge,
Renamed *Côtes.*

And wait.

Wait
Wait
And go!
On the Jenkin Road, where the seed is sown,
Fair Italy comes afore.
A flash of blue and tricolore
Exchanged, soon,
For yellow.

Now, the only way
Is Essex, my boys, and

On to the capital,
Through driving rain
To the palace!
Mall maul,
And it's here
*Das Sprinter* reigns
Once more.


## II. FRANCE


Return to France,
Where the children play,
And the *grands-mères* bicker and grin,
And the old men listen
On the wireless,
Huge ears pressed close.
And they're coming.
Here they come! shrieks someone, and they're right.
First the swish-swish of the whirly-bird blades,
Then the roar of the pre-show motors.
Then the quietude.
Are they late?

It's time!
Are they late?
It's time!

Behold! A torrent of silver and gold

And colour and light and sound and wind.
What wonderful whistling,
And it all begins,
And it's over so fast, as they say, yet it lingers.
A French memory, once
Every few years.

### III. YPRES

One hundred years since death of men.
At Menin, we will
Remember them.
And for now we will remember, too,
How our champion, fallen, struggles through.
Falls once too many:
'Enough!' the call.
A wrist a risk;
He'll end it all.
'Enough!' This time
It's gone too far –
Dismounts,
Remounts
The waiting car.

And for the rest?
Those terrible stones!
The sound of rattling
Knuckle bones –

A personal sound
Amid the din.
Then – Boom! – the sound
Of a well-won win.

A worthy champion,
Every day,
Displays panache,
To win the stage. They
Lay it on the line –
No guts, no glory,
No long-haul plan –
A short-term story.

*Mais les-voilà!* The French, *en tête* –
Long overdue,
Lest we forget
They're one year shy
Of thirty years
Since 'Badger time'
And joyful tears.
And they come:
Brown-shorted cavalry!
They come led first by
Kadri.
And provide in white,
The gaming French,
A Pinot blanc:

What sweet revenge.
Post decades
Lived in tedium:
*Deux Français sur le podium!*

Less thrill our friend,
*Conquistador,*
Whose Bastille crash
Ends his onslaught.
His Russian-Danish-Spanish Armada
Left rudderless,
Their race now harder.
Without a goal –
Without a head,
Left now behind
On the road he bled.

And another day is done.

### IV. THE NORWEGIAN, PART I

The bunch sprint thunders –
Buffalo.
Torn band of brothers,
Each the same goal.
Squeezing through gaps,
Unopened doors.
And 'I've finally done it!'

A Viking roars.

'Back home I hope they'll party!'
What, like it's 1999?
Ha! The first of the winner-less Tours.
Damned spot; blight of our time.

### V. THE MOUNTAINS

The mountains!
And en route to summits,
In huddled groups,
The watchers wait. It's
Here the riders
Creep, quite slow.
On melting roads,
Stars of the show
Toil over barren,
Burned waste land;
Accursed watchers
Close at hand.
In coloured cloth,
Performing clowns –
Water squirted,
Gurns abound.
This mask of pain
The face adorns,
Soundtracked by the diddle-iddle-iddle-iddle-iddle

Of comedy car horns.

Ah, the Italian:
Yellow peril, *campione*.
What hope do the others have now?
The podium? 'First loser.'
Slow down, Italian –
Don't you know what they'll ask you?
But were the others still here,
They'd have gone even faster.
'Needed as much time as I could get!'
He cried.
You've done that, mate –
You've done that, all right.

## VI. THE NORWEGIAN, PART II

'Twixt Alps and Pyrenees,
Respite,
Of sorts, at least:
Continued fight.
Gladiators,
All bound for Nîmes,
Arena finish to
Stage 15:
Fast man from Norway
First again;
Grabbed at the expense

Of a Kiwi win.
Two dozen metres
Short; pulled back –
A classy try,
That long attack!

## VII. THE FINAL WEEK

They lay their heads
In Carcassonne:
One day's repose;
Then they're gone.
A solo feat:
Australian!
In the spa town:
Bagnères de Luchon.

Oh, Tourmalet! Oh, Hautacam!
A win confirmed
For 'The Shark' who came
From Messina seeking victory,
And sealed the deal
In the Pyrenees.

Water, water, everywhere –
Redemption flowing in,
In Bergerac, a lone attack
Succeeds and takes the win:

The Kiwi loss,
In that Nîmes town,
Redeemed by one
*aus Litauen.*

'Pon Paris's grand avenue,
The fairer sex descend,
And followed soon, on laps the same,
Weakened men attend.

Triumphant Arc!
A battle won!
This final surge,
And then it's done.
*Das Sprinter!*
Elysées king again!
The fastest finisher,
The best of men
Who, exhausted now,
Collapse with beers,
And loved ones, crying,
Claps and cheers.

So to the winners,
The bulging purse:
Best sprinter, best climber.
Third, second, first.
In summertime Paris

Endeth our poem.
Three weeks completed,
And the crowds head home.

And the day is done.

---

**Ellis Bacon** is the co-editor, along with Lionel Birnie, of the Cycling Anthology series, and has been writing about bike racing for a living since joining *Procycling* magazine as deputy editor in 2003. He has since written for a number of other cycling publications, and, after going freelance in 2012, has concentrated more on writing books. Those include *Mapping Le Tour* and the translation of Bjarne Riis's autobiography, *Riis: Stages of Light and Dark*, from Danish into English. His latest book is *Great British Cycling: The History of British Bike Racing, 1868–2014*, published by Bantam Press.

# 5

Before Team Sky conquered the Tour de France, it had felt like British teams had to overcome insurmountable odds just to compete with the rest of Europe.

The Linda McCartney Foods team got closer than most. In 2000, they rode the Giro d'Italia, and won a stage, on a journey that looked destined to take them to the Tour.

But, like Icarus, the team had wings held together with wax and, after getting close enough to the sun to feel its heat, the end brought about a spectacular fall. **Lionel Birnie** explains.

# LINDA McCARTNEY ON TOUR

## LIONEL BIRNIE

Leeds. Saturday, 5 July 2014. It feels like the apotheosis for cycling in Great Britain. Christian Prudhomme, the boss of the Tour de France, will later describe it as the grandest *Grand Départ*. Yes, London was immense in 2007 but if you strolled a couple of streets away from where the action was taking place, the city was carrying on as usual. Here, it feels like everyone is heading in the same direction, such is the Tour's magnetism.

Of course, British riders had won the two previous editions of the race. I took a moment to stand still and watch the activity swirl around me as the team buses started to roll into town like some crazy circus that'll only be here for an hour or so before moving on. I saw a young boy, probably about seven years old, in a Team Sky jersey, holding his dad's hand, his eyes wide, his mouth half open, struggling to take it all in.

I watched as the fleet of Sky's imposing black Jaguar cars swept in and parked up neatly in a row. I walked up the hill to where the Australian Orica-GreenEdge team had parked up and earwigged as

Neil Stephens, their sports director, explained to a bunch of VIPs how the day's stage would turn out. I saw Charly Wegelius, a sports director with the Garmin-Sharp team, talk casually to one of his riders. He grew up not far from here and part of the next day's stage will cover the roads he cycled on his way to school. Then I saw Max Sciandri get out of the BMC Racing bus and wave to Dave Brailsford, the architect of so much of British cycling's success. Later on in the day I saw Dave McKenzie and Matt Stephens rushing about, microphones in hand, cameramen in tow, going about their work as broadcasters on the Tour.

It wasn't until I had a moment to think that I realised I'd been standing in some sort of cycling version of one of those Rock Family Trees, where members from different groups swap places and form new bands. I realised that something connected all of them, all of this, and drew a line back not just a decade or more to the turn of the century but further back than that. They all had something in common. The Linda McCartney Pro Cycling Team.

\* \* \*

The phrase 'aim for the moon and you might land among the stars' could have been invented for Julian Clark. In the 1980s he had been one of the leading lights on the British motocross scene but a bad crash

left him with two blood clots on the brain and in a
serious condition. It was one crash too many and so
he retired from motocross and took up triathlon. It
wasn't long before he dropped the swimming and running to focus on the discipline he enjoyed most. Clark
quickly adapted to riding a bike without an engine.
He was fit, strong and competitive blood still filled
his veins so in 1997 he took out a British Cycling
Federation racing licence and entered some local
amateur events. He started in the Surrey League, taking part in handicap races, where the lower category
riders set off ahead of the stronger, more experienced
competitors and try to stay away for as long as possible, then try to cling on if they get caught.

Clark did not pedal with much finesse – one former teammate said his style brought to mind a man
trying to kickstart a motorbike with a dead engine –
but he was dogged and refused to give in. He finished
ninth in his first race with elite level riders and by the
end of the 1997 season had been well and truly bitten
by the cycling bug.

Despite having ridden only half a dozen amateur
races with club stalwarts and juniors, Clark did not
spend the winter pondering how he could move up
from the lowest fourth-category ranking to third category. He was dreaming much bigger than that.

Just six months later, in May 1998, he would line
up alongside Chris Boardman and Stuart O'Grady of

the GAN team, Neil Stephens of Festina and George Hincapie of US Postal Service and the rest of the professional field at the PruTour.

The idea hit him, Eureka-style, in the frozen food aisle at his local supermarket. He saw boxes of Linda McCartney's vegetarian food and it suddenly occurred to him that the company would be the ideal sponsor for a professional cycling team. Vegetarianism and cycling both chimed with a healthy lifestyle.

That night, Clark and his wife Tracie stayed up until the sun came up putting together their pitch. Clark didn't know much about cycling but in the short period of time he'd been racing, he'd been like a sponge, asking more experienced riders about the sport, reading magazines, learning about the Tour de France. And he summoned all his knowledge of motocross, of how to appeal to would-be sponsors, how to paint a picture appealing enough for a company CEO to want to step into. Motocross teams relied on bike manufacturers, equipment suppliers, oil companies and the like for their backing. Cycling teams also needed lots of expensive equipment, cars, a truck, a minibus or camper van and all that would be a lot easier to get hold of if he could attract a major sponsor.

And what about the name? Linda McCartney Foods. That was massive with its implied association with Sir Paul McCartney and by extension The Beatles, the greatest rock and roll band Britain had ever produced. If he could pull this off, Clark felt, they had something they could sell to the world. His charisma and persistence got him through the door, his passion and vision captured the imagination. If Clark was anything, he was a salesman.

The problem was that by the time Linda McCartney Foods, or more to the point its parent company United Biscuits, finally sanctioned the deal 1998 was already a couple of months old. The British cycling season was underway and all the best riders had been snapped up, many of them by a so-called 'super team', Brite.

All winter Clark had been forced to work under a cover of secrecy, although that wasn't too hard because no one knew him anyway. Coming to the sport from outside gave him an advantage. He wasn't restricted by the glass ceiling that seemed to sit over British cycling like low cloud. Over the years a handful of people in each generation had managed to smash their way through – people like Tom Simpson, Barry Hoban, Sean Yates and Robert Millar – but British riders found their progress in Europe hindered. Many promising riders had gone across the Channel only to find that riding there, in such a high level of competition, felt like their back brake was rubbing. In the 1980s, the ANC-Halfords team made a decent fist of it, making it to the Tour de France in 1987. The ANC-Halfords team was led by a dreamer, a charismatic visionary called Tony Capper.

Capper was, in every sense, a larger-than-life character. He wore his heart on his sleeve and his lunch on his shirt, which strained over a huge stomach. He wedged himself into the team car and could eat from the neutralised zone to the *flamme rouge*. He never truly understood racing and had an unhappy knack of criticising his riders for failing to get into a 'soft' break that had gone clear at sixty kilometres an hour, but he loved his boys and, by hook or by crook, he got them to the Tour de France before the house of cards collapsed.

Physically, Clark could not have been more different to Capper. He was slight, wiry, like a little bird but with a steely determination. When I first met him he struck me as being like a cross between a magpie and a chameleon, with his eyes darting about in search of something shiny and his personality ready to shift subtly to suit the company he was in. And he was a visionary, a dreamer, no doubt about that.

How else could Clark have persuaded Linda McCartney Foods and Linda and Sir Paul themselves to back a cycling team led by Mark Walsham, a gritty, powerful sprinter from Chesterfield but hardly the Mark Cavendish of his day, and five relative unknowns? Walsham was one of the star attractions of the 1980s cycling boom but by now he was thirty-five and beginning to fade. The other riders were Simon Cope, Rob Reynolds-Jones, Scott Gamble,

Neil Hoban and Clark himself. When the team registered with the Union Cycliste Internationale, the
sport's governing body, Clark was automatically ele-
vated from fourth category to elite level and became
eligible to ride some of the biggest races in the world,
despite being a rookie who had barely twenty hours of
racing experience in his legs.

Such was the cloak of secrecy that shrouded the
team's birth it took the British cycling scene by surprise when, a couple of days before the Grand Prix of
Essex, the opening round of the season-long Premier
Calendar series, the Linda McCartney squad was
unveiled. Just two days before the race the team's bikes
and jerseys arrived. The jerseys had been designed
by Stella McCartney, Sir Paul and Linda's daughter,
and featured the logo 'Linda McCartney on Tour'.
The day before the GP of Essex, the squad visited Sir
Paul's studio at his estate in the Sussex countryside.
While there, Sir Paul showed the riders all his musical
instruments and recording studio, played a few songs
and asked a bit about cycling. Sport is not without
its famous, multi-millionaire benefactors but this was
extraordinary, akin to Sir Paul McCartney deciding to
sponsor his local non-league football club, while the
team's manager had his eyes set on the FA Cup final
and Europe. Sir Paul insisted the team have the words
'Clean Machine' on the bikes and even wrote a theme
tune for the team, which was posted on the team's

website. Elton John had refused to do a song when Watford reached the cup final in 1984…

Make no mistake about it, Julian Clark was dreaming of the Tour de France, of reaching the top in his adopted sport just as he had done in motocross. And as the pieces of his puzzle slotted into place he must have felt he was off to a great start, even if the roster of riders he'd been able to assemble was a little on the slim side.

The story caught *Cycling Weekly* by surprise too. Under the headline 'McCartney backs GB squad' was a small article with scant detail other than the obligatory quote from Sir Paul and Linda's publicist, Geoff Baker, who said: 'It was a health thing more than a veggie thing that interested Linda McCartney – it's not as if she needs the money or the fame or anything. They are both just really keen on the healthy lifestyle of cycling.'

Linda added: 'Cycling is the boom sport of the nineties and meat-free living is the boom diet, so there's a natural synergy between these two very good ways of keeping fit. Cycling is also environmentally friendly.'

Truly they were ahead of their time. The sportive boom, the obesity debate and the rise of the MAMIL – the middle-aged man in Lycra – was still a decade or so away. As the old cliché goes, success or failure is usually determined by timing.

The fledgling team didn't exactly pull up any trees. Walsham was ninth in the GP of Essex, the McCartney team's first race, but they were hardly prolific. Their victories were few and far between. But it was almost as if Walsham had the crystal ball out – or perhaps he was reading from the wrong script, one that had yet to be written – when he said: 'I reckon the sky's the limit.'

\* \* \*

Linda McCartney died from cancer in April 1998. She had been battling the disease for three years. After she died, Sir Paul requested that fans donate to breast cancer charities, or to causes that opposed testing on animals or, the best tribute of all, he said, go veggie. The cycling team had already been promoting a vegetarian lifestyle – the riders were all required to go vegetarian – and raising money for cancer charities, and so Linda's death gave the team even more of a purpose, particularly with the inaugural PruTour less than a month away.

After a gap of three years, following the demise of the Kellogg's Tour, Britain had a national stage race again, this time backed by the insurance giant Prudential. Clark's crash-course in cycling history continued. He wanted to know who was who and what was what.

Sean Yates had retired as a professional in 1996 and had gone back to what he knew and liked best – landscape gardening and time trialling. He was approaching his thirty-eighth birthday but could still rip the legs off men fifteen years his junior. Clark wondered out loud what Yates was doing with himself and before he knew it, Yates was agreeing to ride the PruTour for the Linda McCartney team.

It was the perfect arrangement. Yates was a long way from shaking off the cycling bug (he still hasn't to this day), the Linda McCartney team needed a boost of publicity, which Yates would deliver in cycling circles at least, and Clark needed to add to his understanding of a sport he found bemusing in its complexity. It helped, too, that Yates had been a vegetarian for much of his professional career and had ridden the Tour de France without eating meat. There was only one snag: Yates would have to pull out of the PruTour a couple of days early because he had to be at his brother's wedding on the Saturday. But that still gave Clark several days to pump Yates for information. The pair shared a room during the race and Clark made the most of it, asking about the Tour, the Classics and racing tactics. Yates is not always the most forthcoming because he sees cycling as such a simple game. He can be devastatingly blunt in his assessment of other riders. Asked why one rider had beaten another at the end of a race, a typical Yates answer would be: 'Because he

was faster.' But if you can unlock the door to Yates's
memory bank of anecdotes it's like an Aladdin's cave.
He can remember specific climbs and descents, whose
wheel he was following, who attacked when, who
said what. He introduced Clark to the language of
the peloton. He talked of riders getting 'shelled' and
'popped' and 'flicked', of 'putting it in the big ring'
and 'giving it full gas'. For Clark this was all new. At
one point during the race, Yates told him to use the
53x12 and Clark had no idea he was referring to the
gear ratio – he still thought in terms of top gear and
bottom gear.

   Yates does not suffer fools gladly but there was
something about Clark he liked. Perhaps it was his
willingness to learn but it's more likely to be that he
was prepared to suffer. And boy, did he suffer during that PruTour. Six months earlier he'd been racing
against hobbyists who'd drive out to an event with
their bike in the back of the car, blast round for an
hour and go home for their tea, now he was rubbing
shoulders with people who were preparing to ride
the Tour de France, people like Boardman, O'Grady,
Stephens and the rest.

   During the PruTour, the plan was hatched for
Yates to become the team's manager in 1999. Clark
already had big plans for expansion and, with Yates on
board, it would be easier to attract better riders: Yates
inspired almost universal respect from bike riders

for his tough no-nonsense style. Yates took Clark under his wing during the PruTour, shepherding him through the peloton, explaining to Clark when he had to make an effort to get on a wheel to avoid losing ground. In essence, this was an intense, week-long course in bike racing practice and etiquette. At one point, Yates said something to another rider and a gap opened so Clark could settle into the string of cyclists and get out of the wind, thereby saving energy. Clark asked Yates what he'd said. 'I told him you were my boss and to let you in or else I'd lose my job.'

Clark pushed himself deep that week but pulled out on the penultimate stage when he hit a pothole and aggravated an old motocross injury. Nine years earlier he'd fractured two vertebrae. Although he didn't finish the race, he'd done enough to show he could survive and that, in itself, would stand him in good stead.

In June, Walsham won the Tom Simpson Memorial road race, an event named after one of Britain's best riders, a man who had died on Mont Ventoux thirty-one years earlier. It was the team's biggest victory of the year and although the Tom Simpson Memorial was not the biggest race on the British calendar its name resonated throughout cycling.

By the end of the season, Clark was enjoying his new profile as the owner and general manager of one of Britain's highest-profile teams. He spoke of Sir Paul's passion for the team and it's true to say that he did send messages of support and enquire about the team's progress.

* * *

Julian Clark knew how to grab people's attention. He knew what to say to make people's ears twitch and he had a knack for the theatrical.

So it was that the team's new line-up stood shivering in Trafalgar Square one late January morning in 1999. There they were amid the tourists and pigeons and under the gaze of Admiral Nelson, which was somewhat fitting because by now the talk was of making it to the Tour de France in 2001. Clark had drawn up a three-year plan. Europe this year, the Giro or Vuelta next, and then the Tour. The squad would be strengthened as they went; some would make the whole journey, others would fall by the wayside, but the goal was set.

As the fourteen-strong squad of riders lined up for photographs with their bikes and a team car, I wondered out loud how Clark had got permission to stage this impromptu team presentation in Trafalgar Square. The question went unanswered, which led me to suspect that perhaps the formalities had not been completed and that Clark was winging it. Either way, it was a neat touch at a time when most team launches were held in bike shops or hotel conference rooms.

Clark and Yates had assembled an impressive array of secondary sponsors. Dunlop-Hotta were supplying the bikes, Rover the team cars. Yates helped get Motorola, who he had ridden for during his own career. Psion organisers and Zenith watches were among the other backers. Everything looked rosy and Clark said the budget had been upped to £500,000, which was a considerable whack at the time.

The new riders were a mix of British and Antipodeans: Jon Clay, Russell Downing, Chris Lillywhite, Chris Newton, Matt Illingworth, Julian Winn and Chris Walker brought experience and youth and an array of skills. Australian David McKenzie had caught the eye riding for an amateur team at the PruTour and compatriot Allan Iacuone had impressed in some European stage races. Then there was Heiko Szonn, a powerful German with almost stereotypically Teutonic looks, a man who could have been assembled from off-cuts from when Sean Yates himself came off the conveyor belt. A former junior world team-pursuit champion, he had ridden for the under-23 Telekom team before moving to England with his Australian wife. He wandered into Pete Roberts' bike shop in East Sussex and said he was looking for a team. Roberts knew Yates and so Szonn faxed over his CV. 'He turned up at my house asking for a chance,' said Yates. 'We already had the team fixed for the year but you can't beat that for enthusiasm so we offered him a month-to-month trial.'

There was another link to British cycling's past too. Adrian Timmis, who had completed the Tour de France for ANC-Halfords in 1987, worked for the team as a masseur.

\* \* \*

Like many before him, David McKenzie had left Australia for Europe in pursuit of his dream: to ride the Tour de France, or failing that the Giro or the Vuelta. At twenty-three, he turned professional for Gianni Savio's team, Selle Italia.

'He's like a car salesman, to look at and to talk to, and I say that only half tongue-in-cheek,' says McKenzie of the suave Savio, a survivor of the Italian cycling scene, a pursuer of talent, a taker of risks. 'He'd probably laugh if he saw that quote and I don't say it as a negative. People like Gianni and the sport needs people like him. He's probably bent the rules a bit but the sport was letting him bend the rules.'

Savio's *modus operandi* was to register his teams in Venezuela or Colombia, scoop up a load of cheap talent and bring them to Europe. His teams were based and raced in Italy but he exploited a loophole in the rules to keep costs down. 'He'd get a bunch of climbers who would get super results and he'd give them a chance. He'd get funding from here, there and wherever and you have to give him credit for that.

Sure, the jersey was covered in logos, dozens of them, but he was making it work and a lot of riders owe their start to him. He presents himself well, he's easy to get on with, he's friendly and, more important than that, he doesn't spin you a load of bull. He doesn't promise much but what he does promise, he delivers.'

McKenzie was not a climber but a sprinter and after a spell with a Spanish amateur team he was offered a place by Savio. 'My first race was the Settimana Bergamasca and I was up there in the top five with Jan Svorada and some world-class sprinters and I thought I was going to get up the ranks pretty quick. But then I went to the Giro del Trentino in the Dolomites and I got my butt kicked big time. I was back at zero.'

Although McKenzie was racing as a professional, he was not getting paid – not in money, anyway. That wasn't uncommon at the time. Plenty of riders accepted deals that offered little more than a bike, kit and equipment, travel expenses and perhaps some cheap or free accommodation. That was how many riders got their foot on the lower rungs of the ladder before the UCI introduced its minimum wage rule.

'Look, he paid me in kind. I was not on a paid contract but he looked after me,' says McKenzie. 'I was in a position where it was take it or leave it. I could have stayed as an amateur or I could take this chance. I thought I might get to do some good races, maybe even the Giro. But the thing is, he never sold me anything false. What he said he'd give me, he did, and in some cases he gave me a little bit more if he could. It's the classic scenario – you hear it a lot from riders who say, "I never got paid." But the question is, were you told you'd get paid? In my era there were Italians racing for minimum contracts but if they did well they got a bit under the table, tax free. If you didn't perform, you didn't see that cash under the table.'

In 1998, Savio gave McKenzie permission to ride for the Australian national team at the PruTour, then he rode the Tour of Slovenia with Selle Italia. 'The McCartney team were at both tours and although I was always there in the top five or so in the sprints, I just couldn't bloody nail it. I was still pretty young so I guess on paper I looked pretty good. Then the calls came from Julian and later Sean.

'My first impressions were awesome. They were a small team, but growing quickly and they had the name, McCartney. It meant something to everyone. Who hasn't heard of Paul McCartney?

'Julian was a really likeable guy and he was so enthusiastic. He wanted to achieve things. He wasn't saying I'd ride the Tour de France but he said the team were going to make it there and that if I was good enough I could be there too. We went to Paul McCartney's private studio early in 1999 and he belted out a couple of tunes, showed us all his guitars and pianos and played them all perfectly. I remember doing a race shortly after that and I was talking to a friend of mine I knew from before and he was like, "What? You met Paul McCartney?"'

McKenzie won the Linda McCartney team's first major race on foreign soil: a stage of the Tour of Langkawi in Malaysia. Allan Iacuone finished third overall, which was an impressive result considering the severity of the twenty-kilometre Genting Highlands climb. Things were off to a good start.

But back in Europe, it was harder to make progress. Despite the McCartney name, Sean Yates's reputation and popularity, and interest from *Sports Illustrated* the team was unable to punch its weight. Getting the team into European races was difficult. Email had still not been fully adopted by many race organisers in France, Spain and Italy and the old-fashioned way of entering races still prevailed. Send off for an application form, fill it in, post or fax it back, then wait. Faxes went unanswered, phone calls were never returned. When Yates did get some encouragement, he'd find he was too late, that the places had been taken by French or Italian teams. 'I rang the organiser of the Tour of Normandy and got the impression that she was not impressed by British riders. I offered to pay expenses but still no joy,' Yates said.

Over the Easter weekend, Linda McCartney had secured invitations to two one-day races in Brittany and Normandy: the Route Adélie in Vitré and the

Grand Prix Rennes. I went along for the ride at the Route Adélie to see how the new team was acquitting itself in Europe.

Yates didn't immediately strike me as management material. He was a loner, entirely self-sufficient and he expected everyone to be like him. He didn't seem at ease with the mother hen nature of being a team boss with a gaggle of needy chicks to look after. Bike riders on the eve of big races can be nervy, twitchy types, wrapped up in their insecurities and idiosyncrasies. Some want to shut themselves away, others obsess over their bikes or shoes, others slip into exaggerated banter to disguise the anxiety. Yates retreated into his own space and, largely, left the riders to get on with it. If asked for his advice it would often be straight to the point. Earlier in the year, when I'd asked him what he was looking for from his riders, he said: 'It shouldn't be down to me to make them want to ride a bike. If their attitude is not right they'll soon realise it's not on because they'll be riding the Wobbly Wheelers "25".'

If Yates had a weakness it was that he could not empathise with riders who were not capable of doing what he could still do now, at the age of thirty-eight. Often he would dish out the suffering on training rides and his riders joked that going out with Yates was sometimes as hard as racing.

The Route Adélie in Vitré was not the team's first race in Europe but it was another education for them.

I was allowed to sit in on the pre-race team talk. The riders gathered in one of the bedrooms at their hotel; some sat on the bed, others on the floor and Yates stood and gave the sort of speech that sapped my energy. I sat there thinking that had Churchill adopted this approach instead of his stirring 'fight them on the beaches' line, the Germans would have been in central London by tea time.

Matt Illingworth, a strong rider on the domestic scene but who was being asked to take quite a step up here, looked at the map of the circuit, which had to be covered several times. 'Just my kind of race,' he said. 'It goes past the hotel eight times.'

It was just a joke, the sort of gallows humour that a cyclist who knows he's in for a kicking would make, but Yates's face set firm and the beginnings of any laughter was immediately quelled.

Yates kept things simple but I got the sense that he couldn't summon up much in the way of inspiration because he knew what he was sending his riders into.

'Ride near the front and stay out of the wind, especially early on,' he said. 'Ride like you deserve to be there. If you let yourself get shoved out you'll be at the back before you know it and it's ten times harder there. If you can get in a move, go for it. I want to see you participate in the race. If you try to do something but get shelled out I'll be happy with that.'

Later, in the team car, on the second, or perhaps

third lap, we were on a long, straight stretch of road which rose up ahead of us so we could see past all the other team cars that the bunch was being stretched into a long line. I had no idea who was putting the pressure on at the front but as the bunch jostled and jockeyed for position, transmogrifying from a bulbous pack into a thin snake, the yellow and black Linda McCartney jerseys all sank towards the back.

Yates sighed. 'Come on boys, move up, move up,' he said to no one in particular.

As the afternoon wore on, the Linda McCartney riders were dropped from the bunch and for a while it looked like no one would make it to the finishing laps around the centre of Vitré. Each time a McCartney rider was dropped, Yates made a token effort of asking if they were okay before accelerating in a slightly exaggerated, slightly passive-aggressive fashion to keep up with the convoy of team cars.

In the end, Heiko Szonn and Chris Lillywhite made it to Vitré but the McCartneys were in over their heads. In my naivety, I asked Yates what had gone wrong. 'We're not good enough,' he said.

Szonn volunteered to ride back to the hotel – a distance of perhaps thirty or forty kilometres, partly for training, partly perhaps as self-flagellation in the face of Yates's obvious disappointment. Yates didn't object so Szonn pedalled off.

When we arrived back at the hotel, Yates got out of

the car, disappeared into the hotel, returned in his kit, got on his bike and went for a three-hour ride. When Yates got back to the hotel, Szonn had still not turned up. It was now almost 9 p.m. and dinner was ready. 'Where's Heiko?' Yates asked.

Eventually, the German arrived at the hotel having ridden sixty kilometres in the wrong direction, without a water bottle or any food, or a mobile phone. He didn't even know the name and address of the hotel so he rode around, following signs for Vitré and kept going until he recognised a road and stumbled upon the hotel.

Yates slapped Heiko on the back and laughed a sympathetic laugh. 'It won't do you any harm.' Yates would say that. Stories of his 300-kilometre training ride completing a lap of Majorca on one bottle of water and no lunch were legendary.

But that incident seemed to sum up the McCartney team during their first season in Europe. Julian Clark knew he had to take another big step forward quickly, while Linda McCartney Foods were still passionate about his project. He knew he had to head to Europe and make the team truly international. He decided to set up a base in Toulouse in south-west France, close to a hub airport.

* * *

In 1999, David Millar was a third-year professional at Cofidis and one of the most highly rated young riders around. Jeremy Hunt was still a sprinter of some repute riding for the Spanish Banesto squad. Roger Hammond had thrown himself in at the deep end in Belgium and was with the Collstrop team existing on a diet of kermesse races and semi-Classics. Chris Boardman was Britain's only bona fide star but his career was winding down and his salary was out of the Linda McCartney team's league.

Derby-born Max Sciandri was Italian, really, but he had switched nationality to represent Great Britain at the 1996 Olympic Games in Atlanta, where he won a bronze medal in the road race, which was won by Switzerland's Pascal Richard. Having ridden for Motorola with Yates, he spent a couple of years with the Française des Jeux team and now it was time to move on again.

Then there were two promising young amateurs. Jamie Burrow was the number one-ranked under-23 rider in the world, had broken Marco Pantani's record for the climb of Plateau de Beille in the Pyrenees in a stage race called the Ronde de l'Isard, and was courted by a string of top professional teams. In the end, he signed for US Postal Service. After all, who could turn down the team of the reigning Tour de France champion, Lance Armstrong? Charly Wegelius was another promising climber and he rode for the Linda

McCartney team as a *stagiaire*, a sort of work experience placement, at the Trans Canada stage race towards the end of the summer in 1999.

Clark made Wegelius an offer which far exceeded the one being proposed by the Italian Mapei team but the chance to ride for the top-ranked team in the world was too good to refuse. Mapei were setting up a development squad of young riders and Wegelius's contemporaries were Fabian Cancellara, Michael Rogers and Filippo Pozzato, who were also turning professional at the same time.

But the seeds were there and it felt to Clark like the stars were beginning to align. 'In three years' time,' he said, 'I'd like to think we'd be able to sign all these guys and go to the Tour de France with a British leader, a British sprinter, British *domestiques* and a real British core to the team. If we can prove ourselves in the next couple of seasons, why couldn't we persuade Millar, Hunt, Hammond, Burrow and Wegelius and anyone else who comes along to join us?'

Signing Sciandri felt like the perfect stepping stone. It would give the team a defined leader and instant credibility. Although Max was not the most ruthless of riders, he knew the ropes and he was popular with others.

'Yates called me and threw the idea on the table, then this Julian guy called. I'd had enough of the French and I was interested in the idea,' says Sciandri. 'I was at a race at the end of the year, the Giro di Lucca, and I saw [Carmine] Castellano, the boss of the Giro d'Italia. I said: "If I go with this English team, would you give us a place in the Giro?" He said: "Sure, why not?"

'I met Julian. He was easy-going, chatting away and he'd done his research on who I was and what I'd done. The money he was offering was good. In lira, it was 500 million lira. To put that in context, a good apartment cost 180 million lira, so it was good money. I was coming off a really good contract with Française des Jeux but at the age I was, nearly thirty-three, it was good money.'

Sciandri helped the team attract Olympic champion Pascal Richard. One of Sciandri's friends, Maurizio De Pasquale, signed too. There was the addition of a couple of promising Scandinavians – the sprinter and track rider Tayeb Braikia and a powerful Norwegian called Bjornar Vestøl. The team may have sacrificed some of its British identity but this was undeniably a step forward.

And Clark was buzzing about the signing of a former world triathlon champion, Spencer Smith, who tested positive for nandrolone but was cleared by the Court of Arbitration for Sport in September 1999. Lance Armstrong had gone from triathlete to Tour de France champion and although Clark wasn't getting that carried away, he believed that Smith could be a success in cycling.

The vegetarianism was not something that all the foreign riders were familiar with. In some parts of mainland Europe, the idea of vegetarianism was completely alien then. I remember being in Spain with a vegan colleague at around that time. She ordered plain pasta without cheese or meat and the waiter returned with a plate piled high with finely shaved Iberico ham on the top and nudged her conspiratorially as if to say: 'There you go, I've snuck a bit of proper food into your dish.'

Sciandri, the son of a successful Los Angeles-based restaurateur, took time to adapt.

'It was pretty funny because the first race I did for the team was the 2000 Tour Down Under and we had to go to this opening ceremony,' he says. 'This girl comes round with little sticks of barbecued kangaroo on and I grabbed one and I was about to put it in my mouth when I saw Graham Watson [the photographer] and I thought, "Fuck, I'm supposed to be vegetarian." I wasn't but at the Giro later that year, we had a team of macrobiotic chefs with us and I didn't touch one piece of meat, not a slice of ham, nothing, and I was flying.

'When I was at home in Italy, this guy turned up in a van and he said he had a delivery for me. He opened the back and it was loads of boxes of Linda McCartney vegetarian food. I put a load of it in the freezer until there was no more space, I gave a load to friends and family. Luca Scinto [who rode for Mapei] took some and he really liked it. I didn't know what I was going to do with it all. In the end, I was giving it to the dog and after a couple of days even the dog was walking up to the bowl, sniffing it and walking away.'

But despite the rumours that not all of the team's riders had embraced the meat-free lifestyle as rigorously as they might have, they kept up appearances at races and training camps. On the face of it, everything was moving in the right direction. They won a few races, not huge events but enough to demonstrate progress, and then they struck gold. The Linda McCartney team's place in the 2000 Giro d'Italia was confirmed.

* * *

Cycling was a hard sell in 2000. Channel 4 had bought the rights to show England's cricket Test matches so the Tour de France was bumped from its popular early evening slot in the schedule. The PruTour was scrapped after just two editions when title sponsor Prudential pulled out, leaving Britain without a national stage race again. And the sport was still reeling from the after-effects of the Festina doping affair in 1998. For many corporations, cycling was toxic, despite the fairy tale Lance Armstrong was writing.

Although selection for the Giro d'Italia was huge news in cycling circles, it barely registered with the national press. The Giro d'what now?

Julian Clark's concerns were closer to home. In one way, the Premier Calendar series, the bread and butter for British-based riders, was thriving. There were nineteen events, in contrast to just six in 2013, but they were small events. He would often ask what could be done to make the races more appealing. More than once he complained to me that he had nowhere to impress major sponsors. 'I can't take them to a Premier Calendar race and show them a finish outside a garden centre watched by one man and a dog,' he said. 'And if I take the team to Europe, we're not going to win.'

But the Giro offered something else, even if the team got off to a bumpy start. Clark had hoped to make a splash with Pascal Richard, the team's Olympic road race champion. He'd designed a special version of the Linda McCartney team jersey that featured the Olympic rings only to be told by the UCI that it wasn't allowed. To Clark this was madness. He couldn't see why the IOC, the International Olympic Committee, would not want its symbol shown off all year round, and he couldn't fathom why the UCI was being so backward.

Richard and an Australian teammate, Ben Brooks, went home after the prologue in the Vatican city, citing a stomach bug. Later, it emerged that the riders had been pulled out of the race because it was discovered that they had taken a supplement that contained a banned substance and they were pulled out of the race rather than risk testing positive.[1]

\* \* \*

By now, John Deering had been working as the Linda McCartney team's press officer for more than a year. Friendly, bubbly and brimming with enthusiasm, he had relocated to Toulouse along with Clark the previous winter. Sometimes Deering's enthusiasm got the better of him, at least as far as Clark was concerned. Increasingly, Clark liked to control the message, which occasionally gave me the impression that he was juggling more balls in the air than Deering and the rest of us could see. As a journalist, it could be frustrating. You'd get a whiff of a story from someone, ring Deering to find out if there was any substance to it only to be told he'd look into it and get back to you. In the meantime, a press release would arrive in the

---

[1] In December 2012, it was announced that the UK Anti-Doping Agency was investigating the Linda McCartney team. In September 2014, there was still no sign of a report from UKAD and a spokesman said no comment would be made until due process had been completed.

inbox confirming the story and handing it on a platter
to everyone else. Again, the Linda McCartney team
were ahead of their time – everyone does that now.

Deering's passion could not be faulted. He docu-
mented his time with the team in a book, *Team on the
Run*, which gives some insight into what it was like
to be on the roller coaster with Clark and confirms
that when it ran out of control and burst off the track,
Deering was no more in the loop than anyone else.

The 2000 Giro d'Italia reached its second Saturday.
FA Cup Final day. Deering, a die-hard Chelsea fan,
had his heart in two places at once. The Blues were
playing Aston Villa at Wembley, while he was in Italy
working for the Linda McCartney team.

That morning, David McKenzie woke up and he
just knew it was his day. He wanted to make sure the
182-kilometre stage from Vasto to Teramo had his
name on it. 'It was semi-pre-meditated,' he says of his
160-kilometre solo attack. 'We were a week in and I
woke up feeling fresh. I knew I had good legs. I'd been
sick at the Tour of Romandy, just before the Giro,
and had been on antibiotics so I started the Giro a
bit underdone. That morning I had a word with Sean
and said I wanted to attack and he just said, "Yeah,
go for it."'

Not long after McKenzie had attacked, alone,
Keith Lambert, the team's second sports director,
came up alongside him in the team car. 'He said to

me, "Mate, if you keep going like this, you'll win the Intergiro prize", meaning one of the minor competitions they have in the Giro. I was like, "Fuck that, I'm not out here for the Intergiro," and I gave him the death stare and he took the foot off the accelerator and dropped back behind me and didn't speak to me for the next hour.

'In hindsight, that was logical thinking. Perhaps it was smart thinking. Perhaps he was doing two things: taking the pressure off while also firing me up. I felt pretty good most of the day apart from an hour or an hour-and-a-half in the middle where I was absolutely on my hands and knees, pushing myself as far as I could. I probably never pushed myself as hard as that again in my whole career. I knew this might be it. This might be my one shot and that I might never get another opportunity. I was calculating every single second I was losing going round a corner or freewheeling or taking food out of my pocket and working out whether I'd get caught 100 metres from the line or whatever.

'With about an hour to go, Keith came up alongside me and said a guy was trying to jump across and asked whether I was going to wait. There was no way I was going to wait because the other guy would be fresh and I'd be giving him the initiative. A bit later on, when the end was in sight, Keith said: "This is what dreams are made of." I knew exactly what he

meant. Sure, it was a bit of a cliché but it was inspirational. It meant empty the tank, give it everything.'

McKenzie hung on to win by fifty-one seconds.
Meanwhile, in London, Chelsea were lifting the cup
thanks to a goal by the Italian midfielder Roberto Di
Matteo.

When McKenzie crossed the line, he was practically hauled off his bike and given a bear hug by
Deering, who was wearing a blue Chelsea shirt. The
Italians loved it and *Gazzetta dello Sport* went big on
it, with a photograph of Deering grabbing McKenzie
and a piece tying in the football and the Giro. Not for
the first time, it was as if all the stars had lined up in a
row for the Linda McCartney team.

But Julian Clark was not happy. He couldn't see how
things stacked up to make a quirky story. This big bear
of a man in a Chelsea shirt on a day an Italian scored a
cup-winning goal in the last FA Cup Final to be played
at the old Wembley stadium, these vegetarian oddballs
winning a stage of the Giro d'Italia. All he could see was
the lost opportunity to showcase the sponsors. He tore
a strip off Deering for wearing the Chelsea shirt instead
of a Linda McCartney jersey. It was an over-reaction
but it was perhaps symptomatic of the problems that
were stacking up behind the scenes.

The following day, with the team the toast of the
Giro, Max Sciandri almost made it two wins from
two in Prato. He had pinpointed that day before the

Giro started because it was the one that went closest to his house in Quarrata. According to Sciandri, one of his breakaway companions, Axel Merckx, crashed on a descent not far from the finish but benefited from a bit of a tow from the Mapei team car being driven by Fabrizio Fabbri and flew past to win the stage. 'I dunno,' says Sciandri, shrugging his shoulders. 'I was pretty disappointed and I didn't think he could come back from that to win but I ended up getting the sprint for second. But I should have won that stage.'

* * *

So how did it all end so abruptly? How could a team that won a stage in their first Grand Tour disappear almost as suddenly as it had arrived, particularly after another expansion over the winter of 2000–01?

In truth, the problems were there throughout 2000. Wages were sometimes late but Clark always had an answer. There was a problem with the bank, or the sponsors hadn't paid but it was all in hand and would all get sorted.

'Of the money I was promised, I didn't get any of it,' says Sciandri, who shrugs again when asked why he didn't make more of a fuss. 'It was a great bunch of guys and I really believed in the project, in British cycling and I thought we were starting something. I genuinely thought British cycling could be the next big thing then, that all it needed was a little light and water to grow.

'I was okay for money. I am not a guy who looks at his account to see if the money has gone in. As we got closer to the Giro [in 2000] I was thinking about the race, not worrying about the money. I got one little cheque, for about a thousand euros in today's money, but no salary ever turned up. Julian was very good at postponing things. "It's coming, it's coming." I'd get faxes of bank statements and things but there was always a problem. You know, on the fifteenth of August in Italy, on a beautiful sunny day, Julian could persuade you it's pissing with rain outside.'

Things reached a head in December 2000. 'I finally got this cheque for 500 million lira, everything I was owed for the whole year and I paid it into the bank,' he says. 'I was driving to the airport in Rome with my teammate De Pasquale and I got a call from the bank to say the cheque had bounced, that there was nothing in it. I stopped by the side of the road and couldn't believe it. I still have that cheque at home somewhere.'

Yet Sciandri stuck around. Clark promised that sponsors were in place. More riders were being signed for 2001. Iñigo Cuesta, Juan Dominguez and Miguel Angel Martin Perdiguero from Spain, the 1998 junior world road race champion Mark Scanlon from Ireland and a twenty-year-old junior pursuit world champion called Bradley Wiggins.

There was a new sports director too. Neil Stephens, the Australian, was recruited, although Clark reacted badly when a national newspaper brought up the fact that he had ridden for the notorious Festina team in 1998, a fact that, ironically, dissuaded Dave Brailsford from hiring Stephens for Team Sky at the end of 2010.

Behind the scenes, Clark was struggling to keep all the balls in the air. Added to that, the Linda McCartney Foods brand was subject to a takeover. It was being sold by United Biscuits, and its sub-group McVitie's, to Heinz. There was a problem. Heinz couldn't really see the value of the cycling team and wanted to pull out.

Clark persuaded them to allow him to continue using the Linda McCartney Foods name, believing that it would attract other prestigious sponsors to the table. The association with the McCartney name was still a big pull, he thought.

Just before flying to Australia for the Tour Down Under in 2001, Sciandri gave Clark an ultimatum. Pay some of the money you owe or I'm going to call a press conference in Australia and blow the lid on things. 'In the end, I didn't do it, mainly because Julian said everything would be sorted when we got back to London for the team launch.'

David McKenzie arrived at the Tour Down Under in a great mood. 'We'd just had our first baby, our daughter was two weeks old, so I was excited about that. There had been a worrying moment towards the end of the previous year. We were at the dinner table during one tour and Max said, "Hey guys, I don't want to intrude on your personal finances, but I'm curious to know if you've been paid." We all suddenly panicked and I realised I'd not been paid for three months. I got straight on to Julian and in the end I got all my money. I didn't realise that there were perhaps only two of us who got everything they were supposed to get.

'When we got to the Tour Down Under, I was flavour of the month – the only Aussie to win a stage of the Giro the previous summer – I was back on home soil and really excited.'

On the outside, everything looked great. The team's new jerseys boasted two high-profile new sponsors – the Australian wine producer Jacob's Creek, and the prestigious car manufacturer, Jaguar. On 21 January 2001, in the centre of Adelaide, McKenzie won the final stage of the Tour Down Under, the Linda McCartney team's final race.

On the podium, the CEO of Jacob's Creek presented McKenzie with the winner's trophy and some wine and said: 'Ah, Jacob's Creek is on your jersey, that's pretty cool.'

'He didn't say anything else but it was like he was surprised,' says McKenzie. 'I thought, hang on, they're a major sponsor of our team and he doesn't know? But then you rationalise it and think, well, it's a big company, maybe he just doesn't know about the deal.'

The deal, as it was reported back in the UK, was supposed to be worth £1.7 million. In fact, there was no deal at all.

Things began to unravel rapidly. I was working for *Cycling Weekly* at the time and had called Jaguar to get a comment on the company's new involvement with cycling. I found it strange that Deering, usually so efficient with his press releases, had not been so quick off the mark. I also thought it was strange that Jaguar would sink seven figures into a cycling team and then let the team drive around in Rovers.

Someone from Jaguar called our office, having seen a photograph of McKenzie winning a bike race on the other side of the world wearing a jersey with their logo on it, in a national paper.

The man from Jaguar wanted to know who was running the Linda McCartney team and whether I'd heard of Julian Clark. After further investigations, he called back and explained that although Jaguar had been in very preliminary talks with Clark the discussions had ended before Christmas and Jaguar were not interested in cycling, as they had a Formula One team to run.

The next time the phone rang, it was Julian Clark, calling from Toulouse.

'No, no, no, you're speaking to the wrong guy,' he said. 'It's Jaguar France we're dealing with. The UK arm of the company doesn't know anything about this and now you've spooked them you could jeopardise the whole deal.'

The man from Jaguar said there was no such thing as Jaguar France and the closest I could get to finding out what was going on was that Clark had been talking to a Jaguar dealership in Toulouse, one that had no autonomy to sponsor a cycling team.

When Clark rang again he was even more agitated and as we spoke he interrupted me saying: 'What the fuck have you done?' A cease and desist fax had arrived from Jaguar requesting that the cycling team refrain from using their logo and name. Worse was to come. A call to Jacob's Creek in Australia revealed that they had donated some wine for an event the team had held at the Tour Down Under and had agreed to allow Clark to use their logo to demonstrate what a great investment the team could be for the 2002 season.

Within twenty-four hours it had emerged that neither Linda McCartney Foods, Jaguar nor Jacob's Creek were paying to sponsor the team. Clark's budget was little more than fresh air and the riders were all heading to London for a glitzy launch in Trafalgar Square.

* * *

Things came crashing down very rapidly. Yates and Sciandri, who had believed everything was in place for 2001, tried desperately to save the team. The riders believed that the team was safe because of the McCartney name, as McKenzie says: 'We thought, Paul McCartney is loaded. Is he going to let us not get paid? Okay, so Julian might be a bit dodgy but we'll survive.'

As it was, Sir Paul McCartney was by now far removed from the food company that bore his late wife's name. The brand had been sold to a multi-national company – Heinz – who had no obligation to carry on sponsoring the team and no financial commitments to it. Clark had exaggerated the size of the sponsorship deal in the first place.

The whole team met up at a hotel in Bagshott, Surrey, the day before the big launch in London. I headed there too, with *Cycling Weekly*'s photographer, Phil O'Connor. There were a lot of confused people, just as many fevered phone calls on mobile phones, and as more and more riders turned up to find that the team they'd committed to no longer existed, a resigned atmosphere settled over the place.

There were repercussions. Marlon Perez, a Colombian rider, had been subjected to a full body search at Heathrow airport. Pete Rogers, brother of Mick who went on to ride for Team Sky, saw the Linda McCartney team as his final shot at being a pro. He got straight back on a plane to Australia at his own expense having already paid his own way to London. Chris Lillywhite had just spent hundreds of pounds filling all the team vehicles with diesel.

Sciandri called as many people as he could. 'I really believed we could keep it all together but the season was already starting and it was just too late,' he says. 'I left that hotel with De Pasquale. We just wanted to get back to Italy. It was the first time I'd ever been on Ryanair. We got on the plane and I asked for a beer and they said, "Yeah, you have to pay for them." I was like, "What…?" It was kind of funny, really, like the last straw, but we drank six beers on the way back to Italy.'

\* \* \*

In that hotel in Surrey, there was a little moment as the riders sat around wondering what to do. Bradley Wiggins, only twenty years old, his whole career ahead of him, knew what he was going to do. He was going to get out of there as quickly as possible. 'I remember seeing Brad and he was like, "Hi and bye",' says McKenzie. Before Wiggins left, he shook hands with Sean Yates. Eleven-and-a-half years later, Yates would be behind the wheel of a Jaguar team car, Wiggins ahead of him in a Sky skinsuit, clinching Britain's first Tour de France title in the penultimate day's time trial. Mick Rogers, Pete's brother, was one of his key *domestiques*.

And what of Julian Clark? Time makes a lot of things easier. The riders whose careers were paused or

disrupted pushed on. At the time, Clark was angry
and indignant, releasing rambling statements to the
media that seemed to blame everyone but himself.
There was a sense, initially, that he had profited while
others lost out but that wasn't the case. The money
never existed.

The UCI introduced new rules to guarantee a team
could pay their riders' salaries for a year. As Sciandri
said: 'Before McCartney you could say, "Hey, I got 20
million, I'm putting a team together," and they'd say
fine. So at least we changed something.'

McKenzie refuses to bear a grudge but says: 'It
was madness, wasn't it? Absolute madness. Now it's
easy to look back and say it's a great yarn, because it
is. I think I take people at face value and I wanted
to believe because it was a great team. I don't think
Julian did anything maliciously. People thought he
was pocketing money but that wasn't true. He was
living on a shoestring trying to keep it together and
pay what he could. Look, it still doesn't make it right
and I'm not letting him off the hook completely, but
he had to keep telling white lies to cover his arse.
One lie to cover another, then another and then the
lies surrounded him. If you look back now, he had a
bloody good idea. It should have worked. If he was
smart, he'd have gone out and hired a bloody good
marketing person to get us that next sponsor to keep
it going.

'I walk around at the Tour de France and I see Sky in their lovely smart Jaguars and I wonder if anyone in marketing there ever thinks, "Hey, weren't we in cycling before?"'

\* \* \*

Unfortunately the story doesn't end there for Julian Clark. He wasn't just an ambitious schemer who dreamt too big and came crashing down to earth. Not long after the Linda McCartney team collapsed, I got a call from police investigating the fraudulent sale of some gym equipment and asking for any information I might have had on Clark and the cycling team. Clark was found guilty and sentenced to six months in prison. In August 2011 he was sentenced to three-and-a-half years for obtaining almost three-quarters of a million pounds from twenty people in and around Kent who had backed fraudulent business ventures. The schemes included importing motor-cycles and selling gym equipment. When asked where their money was by his investors, Clark used delaying tactics, bounced cheques and produced forged copies of bank transfer documents. He told the court he had sold his family home and was living in rented accommodation so that he could repay £420,000 of the money he owed. One victim got back some of the £35,000 he had invested with Clark after pinning bounced cheques on the noticeboard at a motocross club in Dartford with the note: 'Beware Julian Clark. He bounces cheques.'

---

**Lionel Birnie** is co-host of the *Telegraph* Cycling Podcast and covers cycling for the *Sunday Times*. He started his career at a local newspaper, moving to *Cycling Weekly* in 1998. In 2012, he founded the Cycling Anthology with Ellis Bacon and the following year published Sean Kelly's autobiography, *Hunger* (Peloton Publishing). He also owns an original set of the Linda McCartney team's short-lived 2001 cycling kit.

# 6

In the 1980s, cycling enjoyed its first big boom in Britain. The Milk Race, the Kellogg's city centre races and the Kellogg's Tour had the power to create stars.

A young, dark-haired Liverpudlian called Joey McLoughlin was one of those who shone the brightest.

But when he got his big chance with a top French team his magic deserted him.

And since retiring from cycling, prematurely, he has disappeared from the sport. Old friends and teammates still ask each other: what happened to Joey?

**Andy McGrath** tries to find an answer.

# THE MYSTERY OF
# JOEY McLOUGHLIN

## ANDY McGRATH

His face was permanently crinkled into a grimace to keep up, as if he was suffering a terrible Chinese burn. Yet Joey McLoughlin could resist and hold himself in that fire for hours, then would often spring away and win the race. Twenty years before Mark Cavendish came along with his low and aerodynamic sprinting position, there was Joey, characteristically hunched down on the drops, his back like a humpback bridge, his scrunched face a road map of concerted effort.

Once it relaxed, he was a good-looking lad, carrying a bit of *Streetcar*-era Marlon Brando about him. Strong on short hills yet in possession of a fast sprint, he won the Milk Race and Kellogg's Tour, Britain's two premier stage races, by the time he had turned twenty-three. No wonder Joey McLoughlin appealed to cycling fans during British racing's mid-eighties boom. He had it all at such a young age.

When Z-Peugeot, one of the sport's iconic teams, signed him in 1988 he seemed destined to follow

Britons Sean Yates and Robert Millar to the sport's summit. But life in Europe didn't suit him and recurring knee problems stunted his progress. By the early nineties, he had packed in cycling altogether, a burning supernova that suddenly snuffed out. Then, even more mysteriously, he turned his back on it all. None of Joey McLoughlin's contemporaries from the cycling world would see him for twenty years.

I was just a baby when Joey was the king of British cycling. But later, I got hooked on this cycling enigma, first from the few contemporary reports and YouTube videos available, then from reading modern cycling forums and Facebook pages, all carrying variations of the same three questions: Why didn't he make it in Europe? What has he been up to? Where is Joey now? I decided to answer those questions, piecing together his life with the insights of friends, family and former teammates.

* * *

The initial prognosis isn't good. Joey's associates are happy to share memories and send their best, but most don't have the faintest idea where he is. 'He's vanished off the face of the earth,' his former ANC teammate Tim Harris says. As I talk to his peers, it quickly becomes clear that this is as much a detective case as a conventional professional cycling tale. 'I've

just given you a few pieces, they don't make any sense
to you now. Maybe they'll come into the puzzle later,
maybe they won't,' his former ANC-Halfords teammate and fellow star Malcolm Elliott says as we chat
in his Sheffield living room.

If anyone knows Joey – and where he might be – it
is Vicky and Phil Thomas, his sister and brother-in-
law. One Sunday in August, I head to an industrial
park in Knowsley, the headquarters for the Liverpool
Mercury Summer Road Race Phil has organised
round the estate. A faint drizzle falls outside: about
right for a Merseyside summer.

Inside the lead-grey block, Vicky and Joey's other
older sister, Alma, and Vicky's daughter, Kate, sit
chatting, surrounded by a buffet of pizza, pasta and
sausage rolls.

'People ask me what Joey's like: I say that I've never
met him,' Kate says.

Alma, six years Joey's senior, spent her brother's
heyday living in Dubai, detached from his success.
But when she caught the odd interview, she'd smile.
'He had a sense of innocence when he talked. Some
people try and be smart or play a game; Joey just said
exactly what he felt, and I think that was part of his
appeal to people,' she says.

Once out of their wet kit and full of food, a couple of
Joey's former junior peers, Frank Kelly and Karl Smith,
recall memories of signing on for the dole then going

out riding with this skinny lad, who could put away huge portions without gaining a pound. Even then, they could tell he had something special on the bike.

After Phil and Vicky pack away the racing para-phernalia, we head to their home in Croxteth, only a few miles away from the old McLoughlin stamping grounds.

Born in the Liverpool suburb of West Derby, three weeks before Christmas 1964, Joseph was the eleventh and youngest member of the family. It was soon shortened to Joey: just the name conjures up the image of an energetic, irrepressible youth in need of a little protection. A few years later, the McLoughlins moved to Cantril Farm, a newly built, sprawling estate of high-rise tower blocks and council houses on the Liverpool outskirts. It was the government's abor-tive answer to clearing the inner-city slums: at first, no schools or shops were built there.

Joey would spend hours outside, playing in the cornfields on Lord Derby's neighbouring estate, kicking a football about or riding around on makeshift bikes.

'Joey had a really good sense of humour, always playing tricks and taking the micky,' Vicky remem-bers. 'He was a very caring person; he cared about what people thought of him. He'd show his emotion, I'd say he was very emotional for a boy. I'd wind him up and have to say sorry.'

There were two dinner sittings for this family of eleven, and they ate what they were given – usually potatoes and sausages – or didn't eat at all.

Joey's beginnings in cycling were purely accidental. After Vicky started going out with Phil Thomas, he tagged along on a few Liverpool Mercury rides (incidentally, thrilled by watching Phil racing, Vicky took it up too and ended up finishing the women's Tour de France). Phil would become his best friend, training partner, brother-in-law and guide in the cycling world. What he said was gospel.

Soon, Joey was skipping school every Wednesday to join the weekly ride into Wales. 'Our parents had an idea of it, but realised that he was doing something that he loved, not hanging round street corners getting into trouble,' Vicky remembers.

And by the turn of the eighties, Cantril Farm had its fair share of trouble, as one of the roughest estates in north-west England, with a reputation for crime and a male unemployment rate of 49 per cent. Locals dubbed it Cannibal Farm.

'It was a tough place to grow up, but it seemed to produce a generation that wanted to go out and take on the world,' former Newcastle footballer Micky Quinn remembers in his autobiography, *Who Ate All The Pies?* The comedian, Craig Charles, and Frankie Goes To Hollywood frontman, Paul Rutherford, were also brought up there.

Cycling was Joey's ticket out. Only a lack of transport prevented him from faring better in the Peter Buckley Series, Britain's leading junior racing competition. 'I'd have ridden them all if I could have got a lift,' he told *Cycling Weekly* after winning the 1982 Tour de Bumpsteads. Once he had a regular ride, there'd be no holding him back.

\* \* \*

One of Joey's first senior races for Great Britain was the 1983 Tour of Israel. 'We walked into a warzone,' team manager Brian Tew remembers. 'Joey went up to the hotel window and said "They've put on a fireworks display for us."' In fact, missiles were providing the pyrotechnics, as Israel fought with Lebanon. 'The organisers wanted us to do this criterium by a village that was being shelled. We declined that one. When we got to Tel Aviv, I took the lads out for ice cream. Afterwards Joey, typical Scouser, says, "Shall we do a runner?" I go: "Look around: the owner's got a revolver in his belt and that man over there has a machine gun. You can do a runner if you want, we certainly aren't."'

Joey progressed quickly, as Phil taught him the nuances of race craft. 'Winning races is a technique. Once you've mastered and developed it, you can win at every level. You've got to practise, learn to hold your

nerve and not to cross gaps till you have to. Learning
that timing and tactics is so important,' Phil says.

As members of Liverpool Mercury, one of the leading English clubs of the time, the pair were in excellent
hands too. 'You couldn't go into the club on a Monday
and say you were second. Second? Don't even mention
third,' Phil exclaims. 'Pete Matthews, Ken Hill, Peter
Maxwell: these guys were big winners. We had to be
the same. I just expected to win; I thought that was
what we did. When you have that mind-set, it doesn't
take long before you become a winner.' He won hundreds of races with his canny tactics and fast sprint,
including the 1983 British national road race, and is
still a success on the veterans' circuit.

Joey's hard work started to pay off. He took victory
in the GP François Faber, an amateur stage race in
Luxembourg, and rode his first senior world championships in Altenrhein, dazzled by the speed of the
bunch.

\* \* \*

In Britain, a revolution was brewing in cycling broad-
casting, led by Sport for Television's Alan Rushton.
He wanted to showcase cycling's drama and razzam-
atazz to the public, who had previously only seen
patronising Milk Race newsreels of 'so-and-so from
Czechoslovakia riding along and cyclists drinking

pints of milk. There was no action'. He came up with the idea of a national league of Monday-evening, city-centre circuit races. Kellogg's offered sponsorship, and Rushton's competition was born. Its first outing was 1983, with rounds in Bristol, Glasgow, Nottingham, Manchester and Birmingham.

The Kellogg's Series drew thousands of spectators to the roadside, but the patronage of Channel 4, a new broadcaster hunting for fresh sports to broadcast, was just as important to its success. The hour-long racing format, with regular sprint laps and points for the top ten finishers, was easy to follow, and presenters Steve Rider and Richard Keys gave it an air of professionalism. Another innovative touch was having a camera motorbike buzzing alongside the bunch in a coned-off area, showing how hard the riders were trying.

International stars, such as Sean Kelly, Allan Peiper and Francesco Moser, appeared at certain rounds. When they went over to the British pros on the start line to see what the deal was – most criteriums in Europe are arranged to suit a star or hometown hero – they were surprised to usually be told there wasn't one. The British pros wanted to keep their pride and go for the prize money, so the races were lightning fast from the gun. 'Danny Clark, a world-class track rider, came over for one of the first rounds and got dropped. He was sat in the changing room saying, "I've never been dropped in a crit in my life,"' Phil

Thomas, who went on to win the first Kellogg's Series, remembers.

Rushton also understood the importance of selling the sport's personalities to the wider public. Every round was a new episode: viewers tuned in to see the shifting battle for the leader's yellow jersey; how classy, handsome Malcolm Elliott fared against the latest Tour de France titan, or if the ragtag Australian Shane Sutton had won or crashed out. Then there was Joey McLoughlin, the plucky Scouser, all prominent cheekbones and fierce attacks. 'Joey was box office,' Rushton recalls.

His sheer desire to win could lead to some controversial sprinting moves too. 'He was able to make a bike go from there, throw it here and all the way back,' Malcolm Elliott remembers, opening his arms as wide as possible. 'His interpretation of a straight line was open to abuse.'

Take the 1984 British amateur national road race in Kilmarnock. In a three-up sprint for victory, Joey crossed the line first but was demoted after clashing with Neil Martin. 'I was completely robbed… What are you supposed to do in a gallop when there's a national title at stake? We aren't racing with the kids. Race 115 miles and then just move over to let him win it?' he protested to *Cycling Weekly* afterwards. The irony was that, aged nineteen, Joey was only just out of school himself. He didn't attend the podium ceremony:

no point in going for third place. Well, what would his mates at Liverpool Mercury say about that?

\* \* \*

The Kellogg's Series quickly gained popularity: over 2 million people watched the 1985 Birmingham and Glasgow rounds on Channel 4. Joey McLoughlin won his first round that year, outsprinting Stephen Roche into Cork, and his bold racing helped to earn him the overall King of the Sprints green jersey. He was one of the heroes of a British bunch in a racing boom, as new races sprung up and big sponsors eyed the sport hungrily.

One of these, the haulage company ANC, began backing a team in 1985, and Joey turned professional there, joining Phil Thomas. Malcolm Elliott joined the team a year later. McLoughlin won the Sealink International, his first big professional race, and made a quick impression abroad, joining the breakaway in Ghent–Wevelgem.

ANC became the first British team to regularly compete in Europe, but the riders didn't fully realise what boundaries they were breaking at the time. For McLoughlin and Thomas, Ghent–Wevelgem was just the midpoint of a long drive that'd see them back on Merseyside, exhausted, at three o'clock the following morning.

However, when these young men came together on a big adventure, it made for great camaraderie.

'On our way to the GP Albacete, Sean Kelly's KAS team bus pulled in behind us as we stopped at this little transport café,' Phil Thomas remembers. 'It turns out we were going to the same hotel. Kelly goes: "I'll get in with you, that lot in there are miserable bastards." So we're in the bus laughing and joking with the lads, the driver was screaming and we had the stereo full on, rockin' and rollin'. It was a great laugh; it was like going away with your mates every week. That's what made it a good team, that's why we won so many races.'

This was a band of brothers that stuck together. At the 1985 Tour of the Algarve, Thomas and McLoughlin both won stages, embarrassing the home teams. When Joey was kicked off the race for 'fighting' (shoving his way into the pace line), the ANC team gave the organisers an ultimatum: reinstate him or we all walk out. At their refusal, they stuck to their guns and did some training rides under the sun instead.

Joey occasionally struggled with discipline. Thomas remembers one confrontation during an ANC training camp in Majorca.

Joey and Malcolm Elliott: 'We're going out for some drinks: we've trained hard for four days, and we're having an easy day tomorrow.'

Phil: 'No, you're not. You're the team leaders,

you've got to set an example, you cannot go out. Go upstairs and get changed.'

Joey and Malcolm: 'What are you going to do about it?'

Phil: 'If you go out, I'll ring up [ANC team boss] Tony Capper and tell him to fine you.'

Joey and Malcolm: 'No, you won't.'

Phil: 'So go out, see what happens.'

Thomas was as good as his word. A fax from Capper was waiting on the breakfast table the next morning, informing them of their penalties. 'Joey was livid as well. I don't think he actually fined them though,' Thomas recalls.

At least, by now, Joey could afford to pay it. In a matter of years, he went from barely having enough money for a pair of cycling shorts to owning a house in Aintree and a red Mercedes 190. 'He was really proud of that car, that was kind of a moment for him,' Malcolm Elliott says. 'He was getting along in life.' So what did Joey want from cycling? 'He wanted success, he wanted nice things.' Both had a liking for flash cars and the latest clothes and music.

Although only twenty years old, McLoughlin was already attracting European suitors. He appears briefly in *The High Life*, a documentary about Robert Millar's 1985 season, at the world championships in Bassano del Grappa. It is revealed that Peugeot have made an offer. 'What do you reckon on this Berland

bloke?' Joey asks Millar, enquiring of the team manager. It's peculiar seeing the pair on film, chatting in
the flush of youth. Little did we think that they'd be
British cycling's most famous recluses, thirty years on.

Moments later, riding along with teammate Allan
Peiper, Millar says: 'Joey wants more time to think
about it. Berland's putting too much pressure on him.
You know what he's like when he wants you to sign,
he doesn't get off your back… He [Joey] doesn't want
to stay in England, so he best come here.'

* * *

Joey would soon be permanently racing in Europe,
but he first set about confirming his immense promise. His fourth place in the 1986 Amstel Gold Race,
the most significant international result of his whole
career, was all the more remarkable because ANC
teammate Graham Jones spent the first 100 kilometres
talking him out of quitting: he was tired after arriv-
ing at the hotel late the night before. In the finale, he
jumped on board Claude Criquielion and Francesco
Moser's move to reach the leaders. While PDM star
Steven Rooks outsprinted Joop Zoetemelk for victory,
Joey was second in the small group sprint behind. 'It
would have been third but my twelve sprocket just
would not go in. I only had 53x13, that wasn't big
enough,' he said afterwards.

McLoughlin lived up to his favourite status at the fortnight-long Milk Race, an event that tended to be dominated by strong amateur riders from the Eastern bloc.

Phil Thomas claims that he helped to mastermind Joey's decisive attack, persuading ANC boss Tony Capper to get hold of a race road book weeks before the race – unheard of in those days – so he could figure out where the race would explode. Peppered with short, sharp climbs through the Welsh valleys and coming after a couple of tough stages, stage seven between Carmarthen and Cardiff was perfect for Joey.

'You'd say some people were natural leaders; it wasn't like that with Joey. He knew what he wanted and would probably quietly state that, he wasn't the fist-banging type. He kept a lot in his head,' Malcolm Elliott says. But that morning, McLoughlin told his teammate that he'd attack. It was a decisive one too, forty-five miles from the finish. 'He put about two and a half minutes into three Russians chasing him. I just sat behind them and watched. Apparently, their manager went off up the road to see if Joey was getting motor-paced. He couldn't believe that could be happening,' Elliott, runner-up overall that year, adds.

Even when leading the race, McLoughlin still contested the bunch sprints. It wasn't in his nature to hide in the pack. 'There was raw fight in him, almost to the point of it being a disadvantage, that somebody's scrapping so hard they waste energy,' Elliott says. 'You need to be a bit more focused in your aggression, channel it where it matters.'

The first British winner of the Milk Race since Bill Nickson in 1976 captured the public imagination. The ANC team appeared on *Blue Peter* and Joey returned to Cantril Farm, which held a street party in his honour. A photograph of the McLoughlin family and its famous cycling son made the front page of the *Liverpool Echo*. 'Everyone knew Joey McLoughlin the bike rider, especially in Cantril Farm,' Vicky says. 'He was loved; everyone loves a winner.' Afterwards, ANC upscaled their ambition and budget too, with a serious eye on Tour de France participation in 1987 or 1988. If they got the ride, Joey would be the jewel in the team's crown.

When I ask Phil Thomas about how Joey coped with pressure, he says it didn't bother him. But eye-catching feats, like that lone Milk Race triumph, piled expectation on his shoulders. In a November 1986 interview with *Cycling Weekly*, McLoughlin discusses it: 'Once you get to the top, it is even harder to stay there. People think every time you cock your leg over a bike, you should win. That just doesn't happen. It only comes when the form, motivation and luck are right.'

His focus could easily wander. Thomas remembers one Herald Sun Tour where he was out the back every day. 'All he wanted to do was go down to the beach.

A Belgian rider, Jan Bogaert, I think it was, went over one day and said: "How could you have won the Milk Race? You're absolutely shite."'

The comment pricked Joey's pride for the next day's team time trial: Bogaert's squad were starting four minutes ahead of ANC. 'He went off his cake,' Thomas remembers. '"We're gonna catch them!" he said.' And so they did, in the very last kilometre, after McLoughlin did huge turns in the 53x12, with 'steam coming out of his ears'.

\* \* \*

Recurring knee injuries – possibly caused by heavy use of such big gears – would soon blight his career. Tendon trouble forced McLoughlin to abandon the next year's Milk Race, and the injury meant that Shane Sutton took his spot on the ANC-Halfords team for the 1987 Tour de France.

'The fact that he never rode the Tour de France was criminal. If anyone was ever perfect for the Tour, it was Joey. He could time-trial, climb, and sprint all right too,' Phil Thomas reflects. A trained osteopath, Thomas reckons he could treat the injury nowadays. 'I'm sure he had a patella track problem, a bit of muscle imbalance. That could have been corrected with specific exercise; he could've raced with tape on it and been fine. But those things didn't exist then.'

Malcolm Elliott ventures a more mischievous view. 'Part of me wondered whether he even had a bad knee. I wonder whether he was just a bit afraid of that [the Tour].'

Yet six weeks later, Joey bounced back at the inaugural Kellogg's Tour. The rest may have done him good: half of his team was exhausted from a season of trying to impress the Tour de France organisers, then the kicking they received at cycling's blue riband event itself.

He won the mammoth 169-mile second stage from Newcastle to Manchester, outsprinting his four breakaway companions. Yet Steven Rooks donned the leader's yellow jersey, on results count-back, sharing the same time.

It set up a nerve-racking battle for bonus seconds on the penultimate stage into Cardiff Castle. This day epitomised McLoughlin's fighting spirit: where Malcolm Elliott was seen as the classy one of the generation, Joey could call on seemingly endless reserves of grit and bloody-mindedness. The contemporary footage shows him fighting to follow Rooks on the upper section of the Tumble, his head bobbing left and right, his biceps tensed and his brow a field of furrows. At one point, McLoughlin's gear slips and he has to grind back up to Rooks. It hurts just to watch.

As the bunch reforms into Cardiff, Joey messes up the first intermediate sprint, allowing Rooks to snatch lead-out man Malcolm Elliott's wheel round the final corner into the castle grounds and a bonus second.

Later, with two breakaways up the road, it all comes down to the final sprint for third place. Screaming 'Underneath, underneath!' at Elliott, McLoughlin tears away and crosses the line with a clenched fist: the bonus seconds and Kellogg's Tour victory would be his. 'Two months ago, I was told I wasn't going to have much of a cycling career with the injury I had. I never thought I'd be racing this season – and now, I've ridden the Tour and won the Tour,' he tells presenter Richard Keys at the finish.

'It seems phenomenal now,' Elliott says. 'Again, at the time, I don't recall being that shocked by it. That was just what Joey did: he came out and surprised.'

Before the race, news reached the riders that Tony Capper was out of the sport. The ANC team was falling apart at the seams: some riders never received all the money they were due, and Joey later claimed he was still owed a five-figure sum. But his immediate future was bright and assured. Having watched him beat his riders at the Kellogg's Tour, Roger Legeay signed Joey for Z-Peugeot in 1988.

Phil Thomas feels that was a mistake, since there were also offers from Sean Kelly's KAS and Fagor, Stephen Roche's squad. 'I said go to Kelly's team: they got on all right and Sean would have looked after him,' Thomas says. 'Kelly wanted him [on KAS] but couldn't finalise it till December or something. Peugeot put pressure on him to sign up, so he did.' Joey saw it as a chance to have a free hand, and *directeur sportif* Roger Legeay reckoned he had found his man for Classics like Ghent–Wevelgem and the Tour of Flanders. Joey McLoughlin looked like being the next English-speaking success story on the team, after Stephen Roche, Robert Millar and Sean Yates.

Europe was a much bigger place then. Crossing the Channel was a leap into the sink-or-swim, cutthroat world of continental cycling. But at least Joey had a fellow Briton with him: former ANC teammate Adrian Timmis, who signed for Z-Peugeot after impressing at the 1987 Midi Libre. The wisecracking, chatty Scouser and the shy Midlander made for an odd couple, living together in the Belgian city of Charleroi. 'It was a studio apartment, one big room with two beds in it. You needed your own space,' Timmis recalls. He is frank about Joey's ruthlessness. 'Personally, I wouldn't say you could trust him,' he says. 'Joey was in it for himself at the end of the day. I wouldn't say he'd give as much as his teammates did when working for him, but certain racers are like that.'

The first Z-Peugeot training camp in Narbonne was nothing less than a race at times, as riders sought to impress the management. For the foreigners, learning French and integrating was crucial. 'There was definitely a "them" and "us" situation. A little bit of that's down to you as a rider to try and get into the clique,' Timmis remembers. '[Gilbert] Duclos-Lassalle was the boss. There weren't many cosmopolitan ones around at the time, but it was totally different after LeMond joined.'

McLoughlin raced at Paris–Nice, the Ardennes Classics and the Tour of Romandy, finishing third on a stage. His knee injury flared up at the 1988 Milk Race and he pulled out, in pain when he walked. He spent a lot of time back home, trying to mend it. As another shot at a Tour de France ride passed him by, Joey began to realise the value of making his career last. 'I have still got plenty of time. I can expect another ten years as a professional and I have got to take a long-term view of my future,' he told *Cycling Weekly* after abandoning. Sadly, within four, he was out of the sport altogether.

\* \* \*

Joey McLoughlin was a rider who needed a little more TLC than others, and Z-Peugeot was no place for that. His perceived mismanagement in Europe brings Phil Thomas to his most exasperated, his Liverpudlian accent becoming squeaky and high-pitched. 'That team manager Legeay was dim. They sent him to all the wrong races. I remember asking Joey which ones he was doing. I said he just needed to ride loads of little stage races, four or five days, build up for the Tour, then ride it. He says, "Well, it's not that simple."

'But it was. Joey never needed long racing to get in good shape, just enough to tick over and Joey would have flown round the Tour de France. But no, they raced him to death before the Tour came round and that didn't suit him.'

Thomas reckons that Joey's absence due to injury meant he slackened off the workload. 'As soon as he stopped racing, he lost that discipline and training structure,' he says.

His stint in the iconic, cartoonish blue Z jersey wasn't all doom and gloom. McLoughlin won a Tour du Limousin stage and was fourth in the Trophée des Grimpeurs. He delivered on home soil too, taking a 1988 Kellogg's Tour stage into Manchester ahead of Malcolm Elliott. The next day, to a roar, the home-town hero led the bunch into Liverpool for second place, his desperation to cross the line ahead showing in his left-right trajectory. 'He chopped the shit out of me,' Elliott recalls, smiling. Joey won that battle, but the war went to Malcolm, finishing eighteen seconds ahead of his former teammate.

Also accused of causing a crash during the final stage in London, Joey was attracting controversy for his devil-may-care finishing.

*Cycling Weekly* published an article in August 1988 entitled 'Joey The Terror', questioning his 'devastating, if erratic sprinting style'. Sean Kelly claimed that he wouldn't get away with that kind of riding on the continent.

He wouldn't be there for much longer. First, Adrian Timmis went home that winter, his contract reneged upon a year early. 'It makes me a little bit angry now, but that's how it was. I didn't help myself,' he reflects. Our conversation is punctuated by sighs: there's still plenty of regret. 'Every ex-pro will be saying "If only we had Team Sky [in our time],"' Timmis says. 'Good luck to the new generation. In a way, they haven't got any excuses, it's there for them on a plate: nutritionists, coaches, performance analysts.'

McLoughlin followed at the end of the 1989 season. 'You can't have a knee problem like that in the professional ranks,' Roger Legeay says now. In a ruthless business, why give a new contract to a Briton with a dodgy leg and so-so results when there were ten fresh Frenchmen waiting in the wings?

Besides, newly married Joey was missing his wife, friends and home comforts. 'The most important thing in a pro team is enjoying what you do,' Phil Thomas says. 'At ANC, Joey loved it because it was like going out with your mates all the time. Success bred success, the more we achieved, the more everyone else wanted it. If it had carried on, it would have been a mega team, but the finances blew apart. It went too big too quick.'

That chimed with ANC teammate Tim Harris's
assessment of Joey's career too. 'It probably all went
a bit too fast, from winning local races in Liverpool
to being one of the best young riders in the world. As
quick as he arrived, he went down.'

* * *

Joey's return coincided with a crushing recession to
the British economy and racing scene. It transpired
that the mid-eighties period of cycling hope and pros-
perity had been a false dawn. 'There was always this
sense of anticipation that things were going to get big
rather than actually getting big,' Malcolm Elliott says.

Racing for Ever Ready in 1990, Joey wasn't the
force he had previously been, though he took five second places in Milk Race stages. 'I think he got totally
disillusioned with cycling. I understand where he's
coming from: moving from one of the biggest teams
in Europe was a massive comedown,' Timmis says.

After an apathetic year with Townsend Cycles,
he retired at the end of 1991, aged just twenty-six.
Yet three years later, out of the blue, he was back at
the bike races. Tim Harris asked him to be a director for the FS Maestro squad at the Kellogg's Tour.
For a week, Joey caught up with the old gang. While
his heart wasn't quite in the job, none of his friends
imagined that when Joey drove away from the race's

Westminster finale, they would never see him again. In the interim years, he ran a stables in St Helens, invested in property and was a director of an interior design business.

So, why did this bubbly, likeable man excommunicate himself from the cycling world?

'I think what happened is that when he stopped cycling, he realised he missed it. But he couldn't go back,' Vicky Thomas says. 'My view is that Joey has never come to terms with the fact he didn't get the full potential out of himself.'

Little has changed for Phil, who still catches up with his old ANC mates at charity rides and functions. 'Joey's just not there. He's the only one of the lads we never hear anything from. It's sad.

'If Joey walked through the door today, it wouldn't be a problem; if he got a bike and came out with the lads tomorrow, it wouldn't be any different.'

His exile likely transcends cycling: they haven't seen Joey for several years. They give me their most recent address for Joey, in a countryside Cheshire town, and I go looking for him. I send letters, but it later transpires that this is an old address for him. After exhaustive research, I track down his wife, who says she'll pass on a message to Joey. I'm still waiting for his answer; he must have decided he wasn't interested. He may have stopped caring about cycling – it was half a lifetime ago, after all – but people can't forget so easily, such was his appeal. Fans, well wishers and even ex-teammates, like Malcolm Elliott, have taken to the internet to try to track him down. 'The less people know, the more clamour there is for knowledge. A lot of it is generated by his Greta Garbo, Lord Lucanesque story,' Elliott reflects.

Joey McLoughlin remains a byword for unfulfilled talent in British cycling, yet it serves to remind that he won more races in four years than most do in a whole career. Hopefully, he doesn't look back in anger on his heady time as a star.

Meanwhile, the search will continue; only Joey, who turns fifty this December, can give some closure to this story. But maybe that would spoil his mysterious legend.

---

**Andy McGrath** is assistant editor of *Rouleur*. A former reporter for *Cycle Sport* and *Cycling Weekly*, he has covered every Tour de France since 2010. He is the co-author of *The Official Treasures of the Tour de France* (Carlton Books, 2013).

## 7

The Pyrenean climb of Superbagnères was last used by the Tour de France back in 1989. The list of winners on its summit reads like a who's who of climbing legends, so why hasn't the race returned to allow today's generation to join its roll call of conquerors?

**Edward Pickering** recounts the battles played out on his favourite mountain since it was first included on the Tour route in 1961, and explains why he thinks a return to Superbagnères is long overdue.

# SUPERBAGNÈRES

### EDWARD PICKERING

There's nothing much super about Superbagnères, on the face of it.

1,800 metres up in the Pyrenees, on a plateau above Bagnères-de-Luchon, Superbagnères consists of a cluster of rickety-looking chalets, crêperies and shed-like hotels in a desultory semi-circle round a rocky, unpaved car park where puddles, once formed, last for weeks. And, in case you didn't notice it, the huge 125-bedroom Grand Hotel, a colossal rectangular edifice, erected in the 1920s, which sits on the shoulder of the plateau, its stone-coloured façade and imposing early twentieth-century architecture reminiscent of the Overlook Hotel in Stanley Kubrick's film *The Shining*. It's visible from miles away.

In winter, a few hundred half-term skiers, locals and optimistic foreigners gather here to explore around 30 kilometres of piste covered with snow that ranges from good to unreliable. The runs are mainly red and blue, although there are a few black runs a ski and two chairlifts away, up above the resort, on the Pic du Céciré.

In summer, well, not much happens here at all. If you're lucky, you'll get an average cup of coffee and something to eat.

Superbagnères also happens to be a Tour de France summit finish that threatened for a few years to become a Pyrenean equivalent of Alpe d'Huez. Between 1961 and 1989, the Tour came here six times. Jacques Anquetil, Eddy Merckx and Bernard Hinault all wore yellow at Superbagnères, and if these things matter, it's also been a happy hunting ground for Brits and Americans. The first rider onto the climb in its first appearance in the Tour in 1961 was a Scot, Ken Laidlaw (who confirmed Superbagnères' mid-Atlantic credentials by settling in the USA once his riding career was over). Tom Simpson's single day in the yellow jersey was spent toiling up its slopes in 1962.

For cycling fans of a certain vintage, which includes me, it's a holy place. Greg LeMond won here in 1986 en route to winning his first Tour. Robert Millar was first over the line in 1989 in a stage which I still think was one of the best days' racing I've ever seen. The television coverage that day showed the colour and modernity of the late-1980s team kits shining with the luminosity of sunlight through stained-glass windows: the cartoon Z of Millar's team strip, Greg LeMond's yellow jersey and gold-mirror Oakleys, Pedro Delgado's blue shorts.

I'm in two minds about the Tour ever coming back

to Superbagnères. On one hand, modern fans deserve
to see the race revisit this classic climb, if only so that
it can confirm every established cliché about Pyrenean
roads – bumpy surface, irregular gradient, narrow
width, quirky summit. Part of me would love to see
Nairo Quintana, Chris Froome, Alberto Contador
and Vincenzo Nibali race up it.

On the other, it's frozen forever in my memory in
retro perfection. Perhaps there needs to be an extra
dimension to the old cycling saw, that it's the riders
and not the terrain that makes the race – maybe the
era counts too. Superbagnères is unsullied by the EPO
years – you can run your finger down the list of stage
winners there and not speculate about the viscosity
of their blood, nor wonder about who the first clean
rider was. While some out of Imerio Massignan,
Federico Bahamontes, Jose-Manuel Fuente, Bernard
Hinault, Greg LeMond and Robert Millar may or
may not have played according to the rules and ethics
of their time, none need an asterisk by their name.

Superbagnères is also untouched by the dead hand
of modern, defensive tactics. I don't want to see six
Team Sky climbing *domestiques* lining out a twenty-
five-rider front group up the early slopes of my
favourite climb. In both 1986 and 1989, riders who
would appear on the final podium attacked recklessly
and gloriously early in the stage. In 1986 Hinault,
wearing the yellow jersey, attacked on the descent

of the Col du Tourmalet, with the Col d'Aspin, Col de Peyresourde and Superbagnères still to come. In 1989, Pedro Delgado attacked on the Aspin, on the same route. Hinault blew it and Delgado happened to gain time, but the success or failure of their enterprise was not the point – the fact that we're still talking about what they did twenty-five years later is more important.

* * *

A couple of years ago, I rode up Superbagnères for the first time. It was the morning after Thomas Voeckler had won his second stage of the 2012 Tour in Bagnères-de-Luchon and it was as if the whole valley had a hangover. The dry oven heat of the previous day had been replaced by cloud, mist and drizzle.

You don't have to try too hard to find the road to Superbagnères. There are two roads south out of Bagnères-de-Luchon – the D618a, which bends east to the Col du Portillon and Spanish border, and the D125, which leads to the D46 and Superbagnères.

From town to summit, it's 18.5 kilometres. The only insightful fact about the gradient is that it ranges between minus numbers and 10 per cent – averages mean nothing on a climb like this.

The D125 drags out of Bagnères-de-Luchon, the Belle Epoque architecture of the town houses thinning out, past older buildings, along a valley floor of old forests, old trees, the Pique river snaking between the steep hills on either side. The walls alongside the road have been there so long that the moss and earth have merged with them. It's not steep, not even a proper climb yet, even though this is where Bernard Hinault crawled up in 1986, already well behind the leaders, his legs proving unequal to the task his pride had insisted they perform.

The climb here has none of the charm of the Swiss Alps, nor the wide-open vistas of the more famous climbs west of Luchon – the Peyresourde, Aspin and Tourmalet. It's just a dank, draggy road up a dark valley, where the forest looks a bit tired and sparse. The day I rode it, the gap between the way the climb had always existed in my head and the actual experience was huge. The 1980s-era colour television coverage had given way to a monochrome grimness.

For six kilometres, the road runs parallel to the Pique, crossing to the left bank over an over-engineered hulk of a bridge of concrete and rusting iron. There's even a short descent at the Pont de Ravi, where the D46 leaves and joins another valley, less narrow, the Lys, which runs east to west behind the plateau of Superbagnères.

The climb here is a little like the first valley, only even less pleasant. The road is narrower, the surface less even, the gradient steeper. It's just another mundane bit of tarmac straight up another valley.

At Bordes-du-Lys, where the valley curves round to the left, the Superbagnères road pitches right, with a curiously flat set of three hairpin bends laid so close to each other that it would be quicker to walk between them than to cycle. Then more climbing, pitched imperfectly at the uncomfortable zone between steep and shallow, right back up the valley wall, in the opposite direction to the one the road followed along the valley floor. It's more like a mountain road now, with steep rock faces tipping gravel and stones on to the tarmac and unreassuring wooden guardrails above precipitous drops. It's also very hard going – too steep to ride fast, too shallow to ride slowly.

Six kilometres from the top, at a point known locally as the Quarry, the road reaches the final approach to the summit plateau, with a straights-and-hairpins scramble up, and a consistently steep gradient. Unlike the engineered hairpins of the Alps, the bends on Superbagnères are as steep as the straights.

Normally, there's a clear view down to the Lys Valley floor from here, but the day I rode it, I could see only thick cloud behind the guardrails. Brighter above than below, however. No trees now, just scrubby, acidic soil and unhealthy-looking grass, resembling British moorland.

Round the final left-hand hairpin, where Massignan attacked to win the first ever Superbagnères stage in 1961, then a sweeping bend, right, and finally left onto the broad plateau at the top. And just as I rounded the final bend, the clouds were below me, above me the purest deep azure I'd ever seen, and I could see the last, famous, two-kilometre length of straight road all the way up to the looming Grand Hotel, ahead of me.

There's a peculiar optical illusion here, which makes the Grand Hotel look a lot closer than it actually is and makes judging the finishing effort of the climb difficult. Yet paradoxically, as a rider progresses towards the Grand, it doesn't seem to get any closer.

This final stretch is one of the hardest bits of terrain I've ever seen in a bike race. At Alpe d'Huez, there's a long steep straight after hairpin one, the last one, which ruthlessly exposes weakness. It was on this 500-metre-long straight that Pierre Rolland caught and dropped Alberto Contador to win the stage in 2011, and in 2013 Christophe Riblon did the same to Tejay van Garderen in the same place. But this similar section of Superbagnères is four times longer.

I'd watched Greg LeMond riding up this stretch of road in 1986. Three years later I'd been on the edge of my seat watching Robert Millar desperately hanging on to Pedro Delgado's wheel, even getting dropped here. Then Laurent Fignon, in turn, dropping LeMond and taking his yellow jersey.

When I watched on television, as a teenage cycling fan, this bit of the climb seemed to go on forever. As

I pedalled up the road which had been a central part of my cycling history twenty-five years before, above a sea of white cloud, my arms prickly with the goose-flesh of nostalgia, I wished it would.

\* \* \*

Superbagnères' history in the Tour begins with the 1961 race – a dull affair dominated by the conservative tactics of Jacques Anquetil. By the time the race reached the Pyrenees, the Frenchman had a five-minute lead, and his most likely rival, Charly Gaul, couldn't find the motivation or physical wherewithal to attack.

The Superbagnères stage crossed the Col de Menté and Col de Portillon en route to the summit finish. Though Laidlaw attacked early (an impressive feat, given that just two stages before, he'd finished dead last in Perpignan, fifteen minutes behind), he was easily brought to heel. The favourites stuck together, with a dozen riders still in the lead group with five kilometres to go. As the race approached its conclusion, a sudden storm blew up, with a huge wind from the north whipping the finishing line banner from its moorings, and billowing into the spectators' coats. Into the headwind of the finishing straight, Imerio Massignan attacked and won by eight seconds, while yellow jersey Jacques Anquetil defended his overall lead.

Contemporary reports of the stage were scathing. There seemed to be less reluctance to point out that a race had been boring in those days.

*Cycling and Moped* magazine's reporter, Marcel Longchamp, wrote his lead: 'A terrible battle was expected during the first Pyrenean stage from Toulouse to Superbagnères. But nothing, absolutely nothing happened... What a disappointment.'

The Tour's organiser Jacques Goddet thundered, in his editorial in *L'Équipe* the next day, that the riders were 'awful dwarves, impotent, resigned and satisfied with their own mediocrity'. The first visit to Superbagnères had been a bad one. It was a wonder the race ever went back.

But it returned the very next year, this time for a mountain time trial, starting in Bagnères-de-Luchon. The previous day, Tom Simpson had taken the yellow jersey in the first Pyrenean stage, which crossed the Tourmalet, Aspin and Peyresourde and finished in St Gaudens. Following the aggressive pace of Federico Bahamontes over the climbs, he'd been hauled clear of erstwhile yellow jersey Willy Schroeders in a lead group of twenty-two.

Bahamontes won the Superbagnères time trial, riding the 18.5 kilometres in 47–23, almost six minutes faster than Simpson. Britain's first day in the yellow jersey would turn out to be the last for many years. Jacques Anquetil, a steady third on the climb,

which didn't suit him, went on to win the Tour by
five minutes.

The 1971 Superbagnères stage was an innovative
experiment by the Tour organisers, not often repeated.
The stage, the fifteenth of the race, would be a straight
road race, of only 19.6 kilometres, straight up from
Bagnères-de-Luchon to the summit. The concept of
a short mountain stage with a single climb has been
revisited occasionally – in 1972, there was a twenty-
eight-kilometre stage finishing at the top of Mont
Revard, in the Alps, and in 1985, Stephen Roche
won a fifty-two-kilometre stage finishing on the Col
d'Aubisque.

Unfortunately for the Tour, the race itself, won by
Jose-Manuel Fuente, was overshadowed by the events
of the previous day, when race leader Luis Ocaña had
crashed out on the descent of the Col de Menté, leaving Eddy Merckx to inherit the lead.

But it was an intense, exciting stage. The ninety-
nine riders were spread over ten minutes from Fuente
to last rider Eddy Peelman, but there was no *gruppetto*
or organisation – it was every man for himself. The
biggest group of riders to finish together consisted of
four riders – it was essentially a time trial in which the
riders all started at the same time.

The modern-day Tour organisers have gone as far
as the 2011 stage to Alpe d'Huez, which was only
109 kilometres long, but have shied away from a

mountain stage as short as those of 1971, '72 and
'85. It wouldn't be much of a Tour de France if all
the stages were curtailed and short (no matter how
much television companies and bean counters might
like that), but there's far more entertainment in a
forty-kilometre mountain stage than in a forty-
kilometre time trial.

The 1979 Tour revisited Superbagnères for a time
trial, just as it had in 1962. However, while the format
wasn't unusual, the fact that it came on just the third
day of the Tour was a break with the tradition that
the riders race themselves in over a few easy days at
the start. Modern fans will rightly have seen the opening few days of the 2014 Tour as one of the hardest
starts to the race in many years, but 1979 was much
worse. After a prologue in Fleurance, stage one took
the riders straight into the mountains, with the Col de
Menté and Portillon. Then came the mountain time
trial on Superbagnères, and then another very moun-
tainous stage from Bagnères-de-Luchon to Pau.

Jean-Réné Bernaudeau, only twenty-two at the
time, won the first stage, and wore the yellow jersey
on Superbagnères for a single day. He describes that
day as an 'unhappy meeting with the mountain'.

'I was alone on the mountain for the time trial and
the memory of it is actually a bit sad. All I remember
is my front wheel going from side to side as I rode up
the climb,' he said.

Bernard Hinault won the time trial, as well as the next stage, and eventually won the Tour by thirteen minutes. Bernaudeau, like Simpson, never wore the yellow jersey again.

Hinault may have had ambitions to win at Superbagnères the next time the race visited in 1986, but he went about it the wrong way. He'd slipped away with Pedro Delgado in the previous day's stage to Pau, marooning his teammate (and theoretical team leader) Greg LeMond 4–37 behind. While Delgado was all too willing to share the pace with Hinault, in return for Hinault suddenly forgetting how to sprint at the stage finish in Pau, the other climbers in the race – Urs Zimmerman, Robert Millar and Luis Herrera – all suffered an off-day at the same time, dropping well back and taking LeMond with them.

On the Superbagnères stage, Hinault, in the yellow jersey by five minutes, should have had only one tactic: don't attack. He couldn't help himself, however, and he launched himself off on the descent of the Tourmalet, building himself another couple of minutes' lead by the summit of the Aspin. This time however, Zimmerman and Millar were able to chase, and they brought LeMond right back to Hinault as the race entered Bagnères-de-Luchon. In a physical breakdown that was serendipitously and pleasingly symmetrical with the triumph of the previous day, Hinault lost 4–39 to stage winner LeMond on the final climb – just two seconds more than he'd gained with Delgado in Pau.

LeMond, in turn, had a harder time on the climb to Superbagnères in 1989, the final time the Tour has visited. This time wearing the yellow jersey, he was unable to follow the acceleration of his rival Laurent Fignon, who was having a bad day himself over the final 500 metres of the climb. LeMond had been under attack the whole day – from Robert Millar and Charly Mottet, who'd gone away on the Tourmalet, then defending Tour champion Pedro Delgado, who'd waited until the Aspin to join Millar and Mottet, three minutes clear of the yellow jersey group. On Superbagnères, 1988 runner-up Steven Rooks and his teammate Gert-Jan Theunisse also dropped him. LeMond always looked like he was pedalling five revs per minute slower than he needed to in order to keep momentum going, and on Superbagnères in 1989, he looked terribly laboured, almost stalling as he tried to keep pace with Fignon. Ahead, Millar had outsprinted Delgado to win, despite having been dropped on the final drag, with a kilometre to go.

It's unlikely we'll ever see yellow jersey contenders attacking early in a mountain stage again the way Hinault did in 1986, and the way Delgado and Mottet did in 1989 (Millar, though he won the stage and finished tenth overall, was more in the break to win the stage than to gain time overall). Superbagnères' disappearance from the Tour's itinerary coincided with the advent of conservative, defensive tactics.

Will the Tour de France ever go back?

Yes, hopefully, is the answer from the race's technical director Thierry Gouvenou. But there are some provisos.

In the first place, it's the mayor's office in Bagnères-de-Luchon that applies to host the Tour, whether it finishes in the town or at Superbagnères. In recent years, they have preferred to host the finish in the town, in order to show it off as a tourist destination.

The road was also badly damaged by landslides in the Bagnères-de-Luchon summer floods of June 2013, especially the Pique and Lys valleys. Although the road is now repaired, and according to one local rider, is in 'immaculate' condition, for a long time, the residents who lived above the landslides and wanted to go to Bagnères-de-Luchon had to drive all the way up to Superbagnères and catch the cable car down to the town.

Most importantly, there are also some problems with weak bridges on the lower part of the climb.

According to Gouvenou, the Tour can't go back until two of the bridges on the route are strengthened in order to support the weight of the lorries which carry the finish area's technical equipment.

'Once the bridges are reinforced, we'll look at using Superbagnères again,' he said. 'I know that there is real will from the town of Luchon to return there.'

The climb isn't off limits to bike races. The Route du Sud in 2008, won by Dan Martin, had a stage to Superbagnères. It also featured in amateur race Ronde de l'Isarde, in 2011. Kenny Elissonde, now a professional rider with Francaise des Jeux and a stage winner at the Vuelta a España, won both the stage and the overall.

Elissonde is a big fan of the climb – he recalls attacking at the Quarry corner, and finishing ahead of his main rivals Joe Dombrowski and Romain Bardet, and the win was his first major one. He also holds the Strava record for the climb (which currently stands at 42–47), set when staying with friends in a village near Bagnères-de-Luchon. There's also an annual open time trial race up the climb organised by the local club every August.

But Superbagnères is worthy of bigger races than the Route du Sud or Ronde de l'Isarde, and deserves more than being just another Strava segment, albeit a very hard one. A return visit from the Tour de France is long overdue.

---

**Edward Pickering** is a freelance writer and former deputy editor of *Cycle Sport* magazine. He is the author of *The Race Against Time*, which covers the rivalry and careers of Chris Boardman and Graeme Obree, and co-wrote three-time Tour de France green jersey winner Robbie McEwen's autobiography, *One Way Road*. His next book, *The Yellow Jersey Club*, will be published in 2015.

# 8

Those lucky enough to be riding, or working on, the Tour de France quickly find themselves inside a three-week, in fact, almost month-long, bubble – a bubble that non-bike-related life fails to pervade.

But a silent bubble? *Pas du tout*. With manifold sounds, from the mechanical to the man-made, it's noisy in there, as **Matthew Beaudin** recounts – very noisy indeed.

# THE SOUNDS OF CYCLING

## MATTHEW BEAUDIN

No noise.

The chorus is building five thousand miles away. But not here in a dark bedroom in Colorado. An iPhone alarm chime slices through the dark.

Miserable.

It's 4.30 a.m. and the sound signals the start of a deluge of noises of the next month that pound through my head, all our heads, through the Alpine valleys and between the millions of fans.

But the rasp of the shower is next, the boiling of a kettle, the lid rattling off its top. The sounds of an everyday life still and the muffled noises of morning. This moment is brief.

The phone rings, the sleepy voice of a man from Algeria on the other end.

'Sir, your cab is here. I am outside.'

'Be right out,' I say. 'Be right out.'

Wheels rolling on concrete. This is a noise that will repeat itself again and again. Between here and hotel rooms for the next month. Over gravel and asphalt. Bags slamming into stairs. Bags slamming down stairs.

The radio next. Hiss and crackle of early morning's dead air. No one owns this space; there's not much happening at 5 a.m. on whatever day it is. Day one is all I know, of thirty on the road for the big show. It's too soon to be excited, or think, or worry. Thin concern is lost in my headphones, a careful mixture of favourite bands to cradle my brain before it's broken in parts by the drone of a transatlantic flight and twenty hours of travel. Easy now.

### PHHHSSSSST.

The airbrakes of the bus to Denver International Airport break the din of the slow roll through the outskirts of the city, where the factory lights are now odd stars burning out in a post-dawn sky. It goes quiet again. Not for long. Never for long. It is the month of noise. Loud and quiet in alternating frequencies and radio bands and never in the right volume. This is the month of the Tour de France.

The short plane ride to the East Coast I never notice; it's buried in emails and half-hearted story ideas that sound like filler, like boring somethings collecting dust in the corner of a dormant reporter's brain. I've been meaning to do a story about the notion of what it means to be a road captain. *No, that's boring.* Well, what of the fall of Mark Cavendish? Seems imminent. *No, not that either.* Self-doubt has no sound other than your own voice.

*This is the final boarding call, Newark to London.*

Sounds like a jail term, more than anything. Newark to London. Now the white-grey noise of the plane, the piping of the air into the chamber, the *hmmmmmm* of resting and eager engines, the light rattle of the plastic windows. All the sound of something waiting to happen with great force that is taken completely for granted.

What is the sound of something waiting to happen?

Soon the air is a blanket in which we are deeply folded. Quiet on a plane is different than any other quiet. The rattle of a beverage cart approaches, the glass teetering of mini-bottles lined up like soldiers waiting to fall. My neighbour's head falls on my shoulder.

'Gin and tonic. Two gins, one bottle of tonic.' Twist, crack, fizz, the loud smashing and echo of ice into teeth. Bad habit, chewing on ice. 'Maybe another.'

## WELCOME TO LONDON.

For once there is a man holding a card with my name on it. Mr Matthew Beaudin. Wheels on concrete again, the shut of a door. Then the real noise starts. Sleeping until now, the wave finally forms. We've been talking about the Tour for ten months. It's been out there on the horizon, the race of all races, the one by which riders and teams and even journalists are measured.

And the noise is already so loud. Orica-GreenEdge rider Daryl Impey has returned positive samples for a masking agent. 'This can't be the *Grand Départ* Orica-GreenEdge was hoping for,' and 'Daryl Impey tested positive in both A and B samples for probenecid, a diuretic and possible masking agent,' come out of my fingers in the cab from the airport.

Add that to the chorus that was already humming along after a biological passport issue side-lined Tinkoff-Saxo's Roman Kreuziger, and the sound of cynicism was already at its normal rumble. Never overwhelming but always somewhere behind our heads.

'He was adamant that he never used doping methods or substances,' a team press release said. 'Through our own medical staff and independent verification the team was satisfied that Roman's blood profile had valid medical and scientific explanations other than the use of doping methods or substances. This was subsequently confirmed by the expert opinions Roman shared with the team.'

Sounds like... everything we've heard and typed before. Fair or not. It just all runs together at this point and the rainbow of reasons turns to only a brownish tint of noise and what comes out of the public megaphone is the static sound of suspicion.

By the time I arrive in Yorkshire, the Tour de France is in full symphony. The team buses idling and all parked in a row, the staccato insults of car horns angry with the worker bees in the road. The murmur of the fans at the barriers and the screams of the Norwegians. How fifteen of them are louder than a thousand fans from other countries, I'll never know. I ask questions quietly; it's far too soon to be loud and fast. The Tour is long, we always say. Be quiet now, maybe louder later.

## SNAP. SNAP. SI SI.

The unmistakable noise of the race-wave breaking.

Riders clicking into their pedals. The subdued buzz-saw of hubs spinning into the air. The peloton and its collection of language courses towards the start line. English, French, Italian and Spanish, German. The clicks and taps and myriad versions of the same word – *venga venga, allez allez, go go* – make up a river of sound that is a constant every July across France. It's always moving and whirring, a fleeting blur of colour set against the greens and yellows of a country at a standstill while a bike race flashes through it. The sight of the peloton lasts longer than its sound; it's seen and then heard only for a few moments and then gone again, fast as a piece of wind too thin to feel longer than a second.

The first week is always crazy. Crashes and groans and the soft *whacks* of carbon and bone on pavement. Visually it's all something to see, the deep crowds and the big sprint finishes.

Usually, it sounds like swearing at the finish.

Sometimes it sounds like the nervous voice of a rookie set against the constant chatter of the veterans who start stages only *after* finishing an espresso in the start village with the pretty girls in the yellow dresses handing out newspapers to the journalists, none of whom the pretty girls seem interested in, ever.

The newbies play it cool. As cool as they can, anyways. Three years back I was a new reporter in France, terrified by the sound of my own voice at the team cars, or in the press conference.

'It's kind of a mess, this whole Tour de France thing. It's kind of a circus. People keep telling me it's just another bike race, but it doesn't feel like just another bike race. It feels like the big show,' American Alex Howes says while sitting on the back of a Garmin-Sharp car, a wisp of hair peaking from under a cycling cap tilted just so. His glasses give his young face a distinct complexity and his voice sounds so much older than he is. I'm from Colorado, too, and I didn't know one of us could have such a drawl.

'I feel like they've kind of thrown me into the deep end here,' he says. 'Everybody just assumes I know what I'm doing and to be honest I'm not so sure any more.'

Most of us aren't sure any more. Some sound sure. Some sound excited. Even the old guys.

'I really only feel my age when I first wake up in

the morning. Then I feel like I can feel every kilo-metre and every race of the past twenty-five years. But once I'm up and moving, it all melts away. And once the race starts, I feel like I'm still twenty-five and excited to be there. Being in the race never gets old and is always a great feeling,' Chris Horner tells me in Leeds, ten minutes before the start. 'I am absolutely excited for the Tour. It is the biggest, most epic race in the world and that is something every bike racer dreams about being a part of. No matter how many times I've started the Tour now, it is always exciting and I can't wait for the start.'

No one can. The Tour chatter is endless in our heads and in the team cars and behind the buses. Conjecture abounds, always. Soon, we'll have a real race. A real reason to write the things and think the things we think.

And then it happens for the first time.

'It' is Daniel Mangeas. Simply, the voice of the mornings and afternoons at the Tour de France. This is what he sounds like: *LOUD SENTENCES IN FRENCH. ENDLESS LOUD WORDS ABOUT BIKE RACERS IN BOOMING FRENCH THAT BREAK LIKE WAVES UPON MY EARS AND FACE.*

He is the announcer of the race at the starts and finishes; he is blasting his famous noise into the air now and this is the one noise that will hardly stop for the next month. When he is not talking he is still talking. Over the recordings in my audio files, in the dreams I have the five seconds before I wake up. The part where reality and subconscious merge. He lives even there. It all sounds like Mangeas, whose voice sounds like it comes directly from the sky and runs on a generator. He does not use notes to talk about every rider as they approach sign-in. He does not speak on rest days, unplugging the voice that haunts us all.

*LOUD STUFF IN FRENCH IS STILL HAPPENING. AND WILL CONTINUE TO HAPPEN.*

What day is it now?

Sometimes you have to get in the car and roll up the windows and stop all this noise and take a drive. You drive every day from the start to the finish, of course, and then some more. Some days it's more welcome than others; it's the only time you have real control over what comes into your ears. Which today sounds like Bruce Springsteen. It's the fifth of July, and I have a patriotism hangover. Third year in a row now I've missed the booms and cracks of the Fourth in the USA.

*Born in the USA* blares over the BMW stereo.

I love Bruce. Particularly in France.

The race is loud in those days. The smashing of the barriers drowns out even the voice itself. And then the building noise breaks – the sound of anguish and let-down. Mark Cavendish takes a hard fall after taking a big chance and he is down and soon out and the crowd has been deflated like an immense and sad balloon.

When the race is over, another race always begins. The race for quotes and for riders and directeurs and, in a pinch, even a team doctor. So often a job of scarcity, we run now, jog, walk fast, towards the teams. Cameramen are always shouting and running badly and in strange manners. Those of us armed with only iPhones slip into cracks. We talk to each other in the moments between things happening.

*You chasing Cav? No, Gerro didn't say shit. Says he has to watch the replay. He was walking to the bus.*

The scrums on days like these are amoeba-like messes of humans and fans and a smashing of bodies and languages. They sound like fatigued irritation, smell like body odour and feel like a bulky and fattened rugby scrum.

'I wanted to win today, I felt really strong and was in a great position to contest the sprint thanks to the unbelievable efforts of my team,' he said later. 'Sorry to all the fans that came out to support – it was truly incredible.'

If a heart breaking had a noise today, it might sound like Mark Cavendish's hollow words do.

Cycling is always showing its true religion of cruel punishment and disdain for proper narrative. Marcel Kittel – the stage winner – does a press conference in dazzling English in England and he says the right things, which must fall upon Cavendish's hot ears.

Once this race launches it is a snowball rolling downhill. Bigger, faster, each day. All of us hold on tight and look for our places in the ever-moving sporting instrument this movable feast really is.

For the next few days the Tour sounds the same. The routine of click-click-snap-hey-I-have-a-question is already metronomic three days in. The advertising caravan is a constant assault on ears and eyes, with cars shaped like lions and ice-cream cones armed with megaphones. I never knew anyone could be so excited about a French bank, ever.

Generally, it takes something special to knock us from our routines. But sometimes it finds us all, the riders and the writers at the same time. That day came on stage 5 from Ypres, Belgium, to the edge of the Arenberg Forest.

### THE SOUND OF SADNESS.

It's hard to know it, whatever it is. It only sounded like rain that day, a porous and tapping melancholy on the car windshield. I imagined I could hear the sounds of the Menin Gate, where the Last Post sounds. At 8 p.m. every night since 1928, buglers from a local brigade close the road through the memorial to the 90,000 British and Commonwealth soldiers with no known graves, and they sound off into the evening, calling to those who never came home. During the German occupation during the Second World War, the ceremony was conducted at the Brookwood Military Cemetery in Surrey.

Stage 5 this year was known for its cobblestones and driving rain. And for Froome's abandonment and the triumph of Nibali, which was loud in its own right. The peloton tore itself inside out in the driving rain of the north, rolling over battlefields from the Great War and past plain white crosses with no names. It's been a hundred years since the start of a war that killed 16 million people.

In the squares of towns, there are stone lists of those who died in the fighting. Some are lengthy, others much shorter. The land cannot tell its stories, and so the Tour plays its part; bit by bit and year by year it reminds the sport and its viewers of wars and things past. In this way, the arena of cycling is a highlighter to the open book of the land's histories, wherever the races wander.

'A lot of the work that goes into the race is really, strictly, technically based,' Garmin-Sharp director Charly Wegelius told me. 'But also, that's the beauty of cycling – that it interacts with the world around it. We don't just go to stadiums and play our game. I think it's nice when the organisers can build the race around the culture and the history of the countries that we race in. I think it's pretty hard to drive by a war memorial and see those kinds of places without it affecting you. They're really striking places.'

The racing was striking that day, too. After Nibali's masterwork of a GC raid, the Tour de France sounded like something it hasn't in some time, since Pantani. It sounded Italian.

### LO SQUALO. THE SHARK.

This was Nibali's opus now, and it sounded like hands slapping the barriers as he approached the summit finishes at La Planche des Belles Filles and Chamrousse and Hautacam. There was still the chatter of contempt and disbelief – no one can blame those wondering loudly about performance these days – though even that was subdued. Once Contador had abandoned, everything felt somewhat calm for a Tour de France. Never quiet during the day, but quieter at night. The media hallucinations seemed to slow down at least.

*LOUD FRENCH WORDS. LOUD LOUD LOUD VINCENZO NIBALIIIIIIIIIIAHHHHH*. I can't hear what Michael Rogers said in that recording. All I can hear is the voice.

*MOVE, YOU FUCKING IDIOTS*. That is the sound of Fabian Cancellara screaming at us one day in the chute of the finish.

*YOU CAN'T DO THAT! YOU CAN'T DO THAT! YOU CAN'T DO THAT!* That is the sound of Andrew Talansky screaming into the air and at, apparently, Simon Gerrans – what is it with Simon Gerrans, by the way? – after Talansky went down heavy as a car crash in stage 7. He was at the wrong end of the sprint and got tangled up with the Australian while trying to get out of the way. We never really hear the crashes. We just hear the clatter afterward.

'He looked over his right shoulder while I was coming in from the left, and unfortunately just fell on my back wheel. I'm sorry he crashed, but I think, as everyone saw, there was no malice in it,' Gerrans said. 'I don't think I did anything wrong.'

Somewhere during the race, the Italian guy shows up. And he *THWAK THWAKS* at his typewriter. The rest of us are whispering words with our fingers into our screens. Nudging them along gently. But not the Italian with the typewriter. No. He's shouting them right *on an actual page of paper*. I wonder where you even buy real typewriter paper any more.

It seems absurd he's still able to do this, this arcane methodology of creating words and story, and yet we are glad he is here with his *TingTingTinging*. Come to think of it, it may be the one sound in the press room we all may agree on. Well, that and the sound of lunch. Which sometimes sounds like wine into the bottom of a cup and the noshing of free food.

We are in the mountains these days, and glad for it. The hotels are always hushed. Our glasses clink together and the French is so thick I cannot begin to understand it. Rivers run behind the buildings and the roads are quiet. I snap into my own pedals and go, trying to make the cluttered audio on loop through my brain stop if only for an hour. In the Vosges, a couple of kids scream *ALLEZ ALLEZ* at me. In the Pyrenees up the Col d'Aubisque the only noise is the sound of cowbells that clang through the mist. Those bells were the sound of the Tour ending. In an hour, Nibali levelled Chris Horner out of a late and sublime attack – Nibali's got a pretty good memory from the last Vuelta, it turns out – and it all sounded like a coronation. Trumpets should have been playing. They may have been playing in my head.

The rest was mere formality. There was loud, loud club music that more unhinges a body than makes it dance – BOOM CLAP BOOM SMASHHHHH – and the sound of money being spent at eleven euros a beer at the blowout party in Paris.

Marcel Kittel bounded through the club in sunglasses at night, and why wouldn't he? It sounded like victory and the end. Sounded like a hangover.

'Montmartre,' I tell the cab driver at 3 a.m. The Arc is lit up yellow. That is the last thing I notice.

The din of the transatlantic. Wheels on concrete. The turn of a key.

The confluence of sounds flows off me down the shower drain. No noise.

Finally. No noise.

---

**Matthew Beaudin** lives in Boulder, Colorado, where he works for *Velo* magazine and velonews.com. He is a Libra, likes bread and oil, drinks three cups of coffee before leaving the house and has been known to run shirtless through the woods with face paint on. He has since recovered from the deafening Tour and will return next year, with $500 noise-cancelling headphones.

# 9

The track World Championships have taken **Matt McGeehan** all across Europe, to Australia and, in 2014, to Cali in Colombia where the usual pre-event scare stories that precede these kinds of excursions outside a sport's heartland turned out not to be founded.

Instead, the championships in Cali were a celebration of track cycling, a discipline that has been dominated when it matters by the Great Britain team since the middle of the last decade.

Although track racing tends to look the same to viewers watching on television wherever it is held, travelling to championships held in such diverse locations gives each event a distinct feel and atmosphere of its own.

# TREADING THE BOARDS

## MATT McGEEHAN

A terrible idea, they said. A track World Championships in a nation renowned for mountain goats like Nairo Quintana and Rigoberto Uran and notorious for criminal activity of the narcotic variety. Isn't cycling trying to get away from drugs?

Then there was the need for armed guards, the warnings of apocalyptic rainfall flooding a track sheltered only by a roof scattered with holes, thus increasing the number of variables and lessening the impact of the aggregation of marginal gains.

It was portrayed as Sir Dave Brailsford's nightmare, so much so that he decided not to travel, instead spending his fiftieth birthday – okay, pedants, it wasn't his 'real' birthday as he was born in a leap year on 29 February 1964 – doing his other job with Team Sky.

Dark clouds swarmed about the Velodromo Alcides Nieto Patino and thunder clapped prior to the championships, with some training sessions delayed as wind blew rain water into the arena and onto the track. The only wall protecting it under the roof was a climbing wall at the final bend.

An access tunnel was flooded, mops were required to soak up the water and organisers then tied tarpaulin under the roof to guide any rain which might seep through holes and into the venue during the championships. The sheets of plastic looked like giant sails.

There were fears of delays in the racing, while some who shared Brailsford's attention to detail questioned why we were here at all.

For the cosseted track riders it was a shock; from the temperature controlled, air-locked arenas like the London velodrome to one that had more in common with the Roubaix track where the 'Hell of the North' cobbled Classic would finish six weeks later.

It was Colombia's second track World Championships, nineteen years after the event went to Bogota. Some joked Colombia merely wanted donors for cosmetic surgery, Cali being a favourite spot for such treatments. The augmentation of the buttocks is particularly popular and many track cyclists are well endowed in that area.

It wasn't to everyone's liking – the negative disposition of some meant they were determined not to enjoy it – but the 2014 track World Championships were a delight in many senses.

But people make an event and the Colombians embraced their visitors with open arms; the BBC's local 'fixer' (not in the way you are thinking) welcomed his visitors with cans of cold beer.

There were succulent steaks on site, supple salsa dancers and the bike racing was fantastic.

\* \* \*

In Melbourne, a year prior to the 2013 track World Championships in Belarus, Australian models were used at a presentation to promote the following year's event with the slogan: 'You Will Win in Minsk'. There was no choice about it. People travelled in trepidation to the former Soviet state where Alexander Lukashenko and then UCI president Pat McQuaid opened the championships, the Irishman quipping after the opening ceremony that Europe's remaining two dictators were on stage. Just to repeat, particularly for the lawyers out there: it was a joke.

Following that inauspicious start, the championships were heralded a success. A year on, under new UCI president Brian Cookson's less autocratic regime, it was to the Americas that the track world ventured for a third time in the season after two trips to Mexico for the World Cup series.

In Mexico the riders avoided red meat, for fear of testing positive for clenbuterol, and lived on a diet of fish.

There were no such concerns in Colombia, but they had to resist the sumptuous churrascos cooked on the barbecue at the rear of the velodrome until their competition had ended for fear of carrying an extra few kilograms on the bike.

Sir Chris Hoy, in Cali as a mentor of the British team, could indulge, but chose to stick with the team. The six-time Olympic champion was an enthusiastic traveller, but others ventured to South America in cautious mood.

There were reports of riders telling their relatives not to travel, journalists expressing reluctance about venturing to Colombia and, when the wet weather and forecast for further downpours arrived, there were fears the championships might be postponed, or even cancelled altogether.

The reality was somewhat different as the Colombians fast-tracked those involved in the championships – from riders and team staff to media – through the airport and on to free transfers to their accommodation. The passage through traffic was made easier as official vehicles were escorted by police outriders. Even the few riders who chose to cycle to the velodrome each day – British riders were prohibited by coaching staff from doing so – had protection from officials in the busy lanes of traffic.

The doom-mongerers begging for the torrential rain which would curtail competition were disappointed, but the racing proved spectacular, with upsets aplenty, triumph, failure and controversy.

* * *

When the track world comes together, it's like having the fair or the circus in town.

Sometimes few care. The 2009 event in Pruszkow, an industrial suburb of Warsaw, went by largely unnoticed by local residents.

On other occasions an informed crowd absorbs every second of the action, such as in Manchester in 2008, where it helped that there was partisan success.

In Apeldoorn in 2011, it seemed like half of Holland had cycled to the velodrome to indulge in Dutch beer and watch the racing.

Everyone knows everyone. The riders know each other from regular competition; the coaches and team staff have been rivals for longer than many of the riders; there are even family connections with Shane Sutton leading the British team and his brother Gary a key figure in the Australian set-up.

The officials are familiar and even the media are a regular band of followers, reporting on every revolution of the events.

The tigers – to stretch the metaphor – are the male sprinters, particularly those who engage in the individual sprint.

It is a gladiatorial duel, a macho-contest of the alpha males of the track world.

The riders prowl on their road bikes around the track centre, circling like caged tigers before being let loose in the Big Top, where they eyeball each other before exploiting any weakness with a ruthless manoeuvre.

Britain has won the last two Olympics in the event, through Sir Chris Hoy in 2008 and Jason Kenny in 2012, but has enjoyed little success in between.

There are times when Kenny can appear cowed by his opponent and all-too-infrequent occasions when he has been the supreme leader.

Kenny, perhaps more than most in the British team, has a cyclical approach to performance, peaking every four years and having long lulls in between.

The Lancastrian gave Grégory Baugé further cause to be bewildered in Cali in a display that summed up the malaise of Britain's men.

Frenchman Baugé had been the dominant force in men's sprinting since winning the 2009 world sprint title, crossing the line with a primeval roar.

He successfully defended the rainbow jersey in 2010 and reclaimed the top spot on the podium in 2012 having been stripped of the 2011 crown and handed a short suspension for missing three out-of-competition doping tests.

Thanks to his second place in 2011, Kenny inherited the rainbow jersey, although he was presented with a junior one instead in a bizarre, low-key ceremony in the bowels of the London Velodrome at the Olympic test event six weeks prior to the Melbourne World Championships.

After dominating the one-on-one duels between

Beijing and London, Baugé could not comprehend how the Bolton rider, the silver medallist behind Hoy in China, could respond to win gold in London, having had a comparatively modest four years.

To see Baugé as the inquisitor – in the same room in which Kenny had been presented with the rainbow jersey – was strange in itself, but there were more serious undertones, reading between the lines.

There were suggestions of 'technological doping' which Chris Boardman, then head of the research and development group known as the Secret Squirrel Club, and Sir Dave Brailsford denied. Brailsford's joke about 'rounder wheels' had been taken seriously by the French media.

The one rider per nation rule at the Olympics – something that will be rectified in Rio with two permitted – meant the depth of the field was greater at the World Championships, although Baugé had not met the desired qualification criteria and raced only in the team sprint for France.

Kenny wants to be a serial winner, but he gave himself a route to the podium full of obstacles by qualifying a lowly fourteenth. The thirteen riders who were quicker all dipped beneath ten seconds.

'At least he qualified,' his teammate and girlfriend Laura Trott would later say, referring to Kenny's failure to advance from the flying 200 metres in the previous November's World Cup meeting in Manchester.

A second round loss to 2013 world champion Stefan Botticher of Germany saw Kenny need a repechage heat to advance to the quarter-finals, where he was no match for François Pervis, who brought the Briton's World Championships to a premature end.

Kenny was the team talisman, although his readiness to lead was perhaps brought into question when Sutton invited Hoy along.

Hoy and Kenny roomed together when they were teammates and are great friends.

They are very different personalities, though. Hoy can be gregarious and outgoing – even welcoming the media into Apeldoorn's Confetti Bar with warm hugs on a rare night out, for him, not the media – whereas Kenny is more withdrawn.

Kenny has come into his own in recent years, though, but any suggestion of the former feeling undermined by the presence of the Scot was categorically denied.

Without Brailsford, Sutton clearly felt another team figurehead was needed.

\* \* \*

Sir Chris Hoy watched the action from track centre in his role as team mentor or 'Mr Inspirational'. The moniker was coined by Shane Sutton, who believed Hoy's mere presence would translate to an improvement of a 'tenth [of a second] or two'.

That did not transpire as Britain's men's team pursuit squad, Olympic champions in London, could finish only in eighth place in qualifying, their worst display in more than fifteen years.

It left Ed Clancy, the team pursuit squad captain, scratching his head for months afterwards and Sutton questioning the commitment of the young group.

They were by no means alone as Britain's team sprint travails continued as Olympic champions Jason Kenny and Phil Hindes, joined by Kian Emadi, missed out on a medal ride.

At least they completed their qualifying ride without coming to the attention of the commissaires or a cheat accusation against Hindes, who admitted to deliberately falling during the Olympics.

Hindes is German-born with a British father and speaks with a German accent, choosing to join British Cycling, in part, perhaps, because of the depth of talent in Germany, who are a team equivalent to Jamaica's 4 x 100 metres relay squad.

René Enders, who likes to do standing jumps up whole flights of stairs or over chairs as a warm up, teamed up with Robert Förstemann and Maximilian Levy.

The flying Germans, with Förstemann's gigantic thighs at second wheel, were beaten to gold by New Zealand. France were third. It was to be the only time they would be defeated in the men's sprint events all week.

Germany were not to be defeated in the corresponding women's event as police officers Miriam Welte and Kristina Vogel triumphed. Indeed, the only concern for Germany's female sprinters was a message on four Post-it notes in a lift at the team hotel, apparently directed to Welte, which read: 'Miriam. Call. Me. [Heart]'.

She did not investigate further.

\* \* \*

The Keirin is track cycling's equivalent of the wacky races.

It is big in Japan, where it is one of the few sports punters can place wagers on the result. Riders wear armour in the Japanese Keirin, but do not in the UCI version of the event.

The competitors line up behind a motorised Derny bike, which usually emits petrol fumes into the arena.

The Cali Derny looked like a motorbike – a 'pimped up' Derny – but it was electric, taking away the aroma that makes the event a more sensory experience.

The Keirin was no less thrilling than usual, though, as François Pervis gave a demonstration of Keirin racing that left Sir Chris Hoy purring.

Hoy is four times a world champion and twice an Olympic gold medallist in the event and knows the good and the bad.

In 2009 he crashed at a World Cup event in Copenhagen, damaging his hip in an injury that forced him out of that year's World Championships in Pruszkow, Poland; it was a good Worlds to miss.

He liked to ride Forrest Gump-style – to use his own phrase – from the front and Pervis did likewise as carnage unfolded behind him.

The thrilling Awang Azizulhasni did not make the final, but made a lasting impression on the competition.

Malaysian Awang, who once saw his calf skewered like a chicken drumstick by a piece of the Manchester Velodrome track, always has the crowd and the commissaires on the edge of their seats.

More often it is the officials who are kept busy by the Malaysian.

The 'Pocket Rocket' spots gaps that others dare not enter and did so again in the semi-final, resulting in his disqualification and a heavy fall for Australia's Matthew Glaetzer.

Glaetzer spectacularly flipped backwards out of his saddle, propelling his bike up the steeply banked home straight to bounce and fly towards the commentary box, where it left some of the occupants needing to change their underwear. Chris Boardman was composed enough to get a photo while sitting alongside Simon Brotherton, the BBC commentator.

The final was no less incident-packed as Olympic silver medallist Maximilian Levy crashed out, incurring fractures to various points of his shoulder, in a collision defending champion Jason Kenny did well to swerve.

Levy resurfaced three days later sporting a sling and a polo shirt shorn of the fabric on its shoulder to give a glimpse of some of his ailments. In a city where there is still bull fighting, he looked like an animal that had escaped death after a last-gasp reprieve.

Fabian Puerta gave the home crowd, with their vuvuzelas and loud roars, interest in the final and he finished best of the rest with silver for Colombia's first medal of the championships.

Kenny was fifth as his former teammate Hoy looked on.

Cali was always one of Hoy's favourite trips as a rider and he did not hesitate when invited by British head coach Shane Sutton in an unpaid, voluntary mentoring role.

The Scot engaged in the racing as a fan, enjoying being able to be at a cycling event without being pulled left, right and centre by requests from organisations, sponsors, fans and the media.

He also loved the atmosphere.

Hoy said: 'I remember a few years ago there was a Colombian rider who won the omnium and beat Ed [Clancy] and the place... I thought the roof was going to come off.'

That would really give the detractors something to complain about.

* * *

Some suggest track racing is dull and predictable.

Rarely is it so, but there is no argument that there can be dominant individuals and teams.

One near-certainty each year is that the British women's team pursuit squad will return from the World Championships with gold medals.

Champions in five of the six previous World Championships with three riders and over three kilometres – a run that included victories in Manchester, Pruszkow, Apeldoorn, Melbourne and Minsk; silver in Copenhagen the only error – their dominance had strengthened with the addition of an extra rider and an additional 1,000 metres.

Yet Joanna Rowsell, Laura Trott, Elinor Barker and Katie Archibald flirted with failure in the closing laps.

Barker, by her own admission, could not keep up and peeled away moments after hitting the front on the penultimate lap, narrowly avoiding a collision with Trott who then had to sprint after Rowsell and Archibald to ensure Britain held off the Canadians to take gold.

The triumph left Dani King, the reserve after revelation Archibald was selected in her stead, in floods of tears: it was the largest downpour inside the velodrome all week.

The British girls managed to make light of the incident, giggling wildly at each other in recalling their narrow and lucky escape.

Archibald, a nineteen-year-old from Milngavie, near Glasgow – the start of the West Highland Way and home of Colpi's ice cream, the world's finest – has a penchant for piercings, hair dye and tattoos. For Cali, her hair was red, white and blue.

Whether the first Scottish female world champion track cyclist will go on to get a rainbow stripes tattoo, who knows, but her win was predicted to be the start of a big future.

* * *

Fabian Puerta's Keirin performance was merely an hors d'oeuvre for the spectators as Edwin Avila thrilled his home town crowd.

So much so that one British Cycling coach – one of the championship's major critics – declared it the loudest he had heard at a velodrome 'inside or outside'. Perhaps he was getting carried away in the moment and forgetting the deafening din at the London 2012 Olympics.

With the sound escaping through the sides of the arena and the holes where water was creeping in a few days earlier and between sessions – for conveniently the forecast downpours arrived, but not while the majority of bike racing was occurring – it truly was a cauldron of noise as Avila three times lapped the field. Three times.

Three others managed to take two laps and seven more a single lap but their efforts were dwarfed by Avila, who reclaimed the points race world title he first won in Apeldoorn three years earlier.

It was a points race performance few have managed; perhaps only Australian Cameron Meyer in recent years.

The twenty-four-year-old Avila was the star of the show, taking his place on top of the podium, yet still smaller than his rivals in silver and bronze position.

Once the formal presentation was done, Avila was joined on the podium by his emotional parents and it was easy to see where his short stature came from. The trio posed for photographers before exiting stage left where they were surrounded by a sea of reporters and camera crews eager to snatch a word with the hero of the hour in a huddle which lasted for fifteen minutes, when usually those types of things continue for just five.

He is a name to watch. Simon Yates, his predecessor as world champion, impressed in the 2014 Tour de France, less than eighteen months after winning in Minsk.

As Avila was achieving national acclaim, Owain Doull of Britain and Belarus's Anton Muzychkin finished with the unwanted distinction of being pointless.

On the undercard to Avila's victory was a one-kilo-metre time-trial event in which two riders went under the sixty-second barrier.

The kilo has lost some of its kudos since being removed from the Olympic programme post-Athens, when Hoy won gold, but remains a pure event which builds to a thrilling climax as riders take it in turns to go against the clock over four laps.

At the December Track World Cup meeting in Aguascalientes, François Pervis set the world record of 56.303 seconds, beating Arnaud Tournant's mark of 58.875 seconds which had stood for twelve years. Both were assisted by altitude.

The Cali track's altitude of 1,000 metres provided a smidgen of support as Pervis put in another phenom-enal performance to win gold in 59.385 to Joachim Eilers' 59.984.

\* \* \*

As François Pervis was making serene progress through the sprint competition, Kristina Vogel was complet-ing her win in the corresponding women's event.

The German was peerless in winning the Keirin,

too, on Sunday's final day, celebrating by telling all and sundry it was an 'un-fucking-believable' championships for her.

It was clear the police officer and cyclist was overcome by excitement after the German women swept the board in the sprint events with three golds for Vogel and two for Miriam Welte.

Pervis had a phenomenal championships, too. There was no roar, like Grégory Baugé, when he triumphed, as if he had expected to do so given his phenomenal performances over the week.

Pervis won every time he stepped on to the track; thirteen times he mounted his bike on the pine boards and each time he crossed the line first.

The most special win for Pervis was in the blue riband event, the sprint.

He qualified quickest, beat Olympic champion Jason Kenny in the quarter-finals and then defeated Stefan Bötticher of Germany, the defending champion, to claim his third rainbow jersey of a remarkable week.

He kissed the track after dismounting following his final win of the championships.

'Three world titles,' he said. 'It's the first time for me. The first time I've won the sprint and Keirin and I did an amazing time in the kilo, under one minute.

'Everybody pushed me and it [Cali] is my second home.'

Given Baugé's comments and Kenny's mid-Olympic cycle lull, Pervis was good natured when questioned on his dominance.

'We don't have special wheels,' Pervis laughed in response to BBC journalist Jill Douglas's tongue-in-cheek inquisition.

Douglas had to be patient to wait for the man of the moment as he appeared to dissect every revolution of each of his thirteen races with two French journalists, neither of whom had a tape recorder running or were taking comprehensive notes.

However, Douglas was not the only female in the velodrome left swooning like Sue Barker when David Ginola appeared on *A Question of Sport*, as Pervis proved as charming off the bike as he was a force on it.

Rather than finishing on the high of Pervis's brilliance, the competition descended into farce when a brilliant 200-lap (50km) Madison proved more chaotic than usual.

Belgian pair Jasper De Buyst and Kenny De Ketele thought they had won it after scoring in nine of the ten sprints to accumulate thirty-one points.

But much deliberation from the UCI commissaires – around thirty minutes of discussions meant the stands were near empty and workers had begun dismantling the event infrastructure – saw the Belgians denied and the Spanish pair David Muntaner and Albert Torres awarded gold.

It was a chaotic conclusion to a championships which should be celebrated as an overwhelming success, coming outside the established track racing heartland.

* * *

There was uncertainty over the track immediately afterwards, with TBC alongside the dates and venues for the 2015 calendar, leaving UCI president Brian Cookson to deal with questions about the future.

The concern of federations was not about the venue for the World Championships themselves, but the lead-up to them, as the World Cup series carried qualification points for the event, and the 2016 Rio de Janeiro Olympics.

Riders must also qualify for World Cups through lower-profile meets throughout the summer.

'The real-world problem was that there weren't any bidders coming forward,' Cookson said. 'The ones that were interested originally had withdrawn.'

It highlighted the fragile nature of track competition and the tender process, which Cookson insisted would be reviewed.

The Briton also robustly defended the decision to take the event to Colombia, to a velodrome some regarded as unsuitable.

'There's a clue in the name – it's a World

Championships, so there's got to be an opportunity of travelling from place to place,' he said. 'It can't always be in the easiest places in Europe.

'What we've got to make sure is when it does travel around the world, it's in venues that are suitable, facilities are accessible and all the rest of it.

'I'm determined that that's what we'll do in the future.'

For traditional track powerhouse Britain, the off-track concerns were slight compared to those on it.

Shane Sutton and Sir Chris Hoy were somewhat optimistic – this was the usual mid-Olympic cycle lull – yet the performance of Britain's men was particularly alarming as they finished without a medal for the first time since 1998 and the early days of Lottery funding.

Despite being his usual bullish self overall, Sutton was scathing of the younger members of the men's endurance squad, while simultaneously calling for Peter Kennaugh and Sir Bradley Wiggins to commit to the track for Rio.

So concerned was Chris Boardman, previously one of Sir Dave Brailsford's leading lieutenants, that he called for the British Cycling performance director to declare his commitment to the programme or to move on, allowing someone else to take over.

'It needs a full-time boss,' Boardman said. 'Dave would clearly be the best full-time boss, but if he's not going to do that, it might be better if somebody else comes in and takes the reins.

'He's such a character, if he's still there it's difficult for people to go in and take command, but it needs somebody like him.

'British Cycling's in a period of change now. Still got some fantastic ingredients, some great athletes, got some great people working for them.

'The potential is all still there. It just might need somebody to pull it all together.'

In the aftermath of London 2012, Brailsford told the British Cycling staff and riders that he would be with them all the way to the Copacabana Beach in Rio, when many thought he would be finishing on a high, like Hoy and Pendleton.

After eight golds in Beijing and London – fourteen medals on the track from twenty events – to repeat the trick in Rio and lead Tour de France-challenging teams on an annual basis, would be like lightning striking thrice.

Brailsford often described his dual role – as British Cycling performance director and Team Sky principal – as one of spinning plates. He ensured all his plates kept spinning and if one was about to topple off its stick, he would reach for it and ensure it returned to a rhythmical spin.

In Cali it seemed the plate marked 'track' – for so long a reliable spinner – was close to falling off.

A few weeks later, Brailsford quit his role as British Cycling performance director to concentrate on life on the road with Team Sky.

It was perhaps fitting that the final track World Championships under the tenure of the man who coined the phrase 'the aggregation of marginal gains' took place at an outdoor velodrome. And it was great.

---

**Matt McGeehan** is a sports reporter for the Press Association, the UK's national news agency. He has covered cycling on the track and road since 2009. Cali was his sixth track World Championships.

## 10

Between 1903 and 1986, just three men had been at the helm of the Tour de France: Henri Desgrange, Jacques Goddet and Félix Lévitan.

But when Goddet retired and Lévitan went with him, a Cognac salesman called Jean-François Naquet-Radiguet took over with a determination to drag the Tour into the future.

As **Daniel Friebe** discovers, Naquet-Radiguet's methods were perhaps too revolutionary at the time. And when he was ousted in May 1988 after just one year in charge, the Tour was left rudderless and, it seemed, almost anyone could turn up and claim to be the Tour's director.

# THE COGNAC SALESMAN AND THE CONMAN

## DANIEL FRIEBE

*In order to fulfil his destiny, man has to believe in it.*
*A crook sells him wind, he loses hope.*
'The Oyster and the Lobster', Jean du Frout

As a child and even as a young man, Jean-François Naquet-Radiguet was never interested in sport. 'Not my cup of tea,' he says, pandering to his British audience. When, as a teenager, he completed the French adolescent rite of passage that is a Tour on the publicity caravan – three weeks balancing on a gaudily decorated trailer and pelting spectators with key rings (or, in his case, Scotch sticky tape) – his interest was purely professional. 'It allowed me to see what the Tour was all about and how big it was,' he remarks flatly. When, later, he'll tell us that he next returned to the Tour in the mid-1980s and the caravan remained '*folklorique*', this is not intended as a compliment. '*Folklorique*' does not mean legendary, charmingly traditional, the stuff of folklore. It means archaic, quaint or, at worst, naff. Which, if we're being honest, is exactly what the caravan remains today.

For twelve months between May 1987 and May 1988, Jean-François Naquet-Radiguet waged a one-man war on what the Tour called 'folklore' and looked to him like crippling intransigence. In the race's 110-year history, there have been just seven directors, and two of them – Naquet-Radiguet and Jean-Pierre Courcol who followed him – account for two years between them. Courcol wasn't even truly the race director, only taking on the nominal title in 1988 because Naquet-Radiguet had been shown the door in May and not yet replaced by the time that year's race got underway with a bizarre 'preface' team-time trial. Naquet-Radiguet is, then, the real anomaly, the mongrel child in a noble bloodline beginning with Henri Desgrange and passing through Jacques Goddet and Félix Lévitan – then pausing with Naquet-Radiguet and Courcol – and resuming with Jean-Marie Leblanc and Christian Prudhomme.

Most cycling fans barely even know the name. And yet Naquet-Radiguet is far from an irrelevance, a short and makeshift bridge between the Goddet–Lévitan era and the modern age ushered in by Jean-Marie Leblanc. Philippe Sudres, the Tour's current head of media, began working for what was then the Société du Tour de France in 1980. He believes that what Naquet-Radiguet achieved in a single year is 'vastly underestimated in the history of the Tour' and made 'a big contribution to tipping the Tour towards modernity'.

Naquet-Radiguet's list of accomplishments is surprisingly long, although sometimes disputed. Depending on who you listen to, he either did or didn't introduce the Tour's *Village Départ*, the first uniforms for race staff, the first corporate hospitality junkets and a winner's podium and finish-line that, unlike their predecessors, didn't look as though they had been commandeered from a school sports day. Naquet-Radiguet also began the process of Anglicisation which today makes the Tour (and indeed all of professional cycling) truly bilingual – with press conferences and official race literature in both French and English – and which continues to horrify certain traditionalists. On the eve of the 2014 GP Cholet, the FDJ.fr team manager, Marc Madiot, threatened to 'shoot himself' when the chief commissaire announced that the pre-race briefing, in the Cholet town hall, would be delivered in English. 'I think that when we're in a French town hall, for fuck's sake, there's something wrong if we're doing the meeting in English,' Madiot seethed. What Madiot, who rode the 1987 Tour, probably wouldn't have known or acknowledged, was that the race official committing his idea of heresy was perhaps less deserving of his ire than Jean-François Naquet-Radiguet, the first Tour director to give an interview in English way back in the mid-1980s.

Naquet-Radiguet's laconic self-assessment is that he merely 'went into a stuffy environment and opened

the windows and doors'. More impartial judges maintain that he dragged the Tour kicking and screaming
towards the twenty-first century.

Born in 1940 in Compiègne – a handsome town
in Picardie which since 1968 has hosted the start
of Paris–Roubaix – he had what he calls a 'normal
upbringing' as the child of an engineer and a house-
wife, in parallel to 'a normal education'. In the second
instance, Naquet-Radiguet is rather underplaying
things: after his undergraduate degree, he enrolled
in and completed an MBA at Harvard School of
Business. He then embarked on a high-flying corporate career which took him first to France's foremost
manufacturer of cooking oils, Lesieur, then to dairy
group Gervais-Danone, and finally to Cognac giants
Martell. At Martell, he broached new frontiers by giving Venezuela its first vineyard. 'They said it couldn't
be done but we did it, and the wine was good,' he said
triumphantly in an interview with *Le Monde* in 1987.
He also spotted a silver lining in the financial crisis
that shattered the Mexican economy and prompted
a near freeze on exports in the early 1980s, planting
grapes and building a distillery that allowed Martell
to clone its Cognac in central America.

In the late spring of 1987, though, the lure of
home was tugging on Naquet-Radiguet's heart-
strings. Once again, one man's adversity was another
man's opportunity when a curious, unique opening

presented itself: an acquaintance at Amaury Sport Organisation, the parent company of the Société du Tour de France, was desperately searching for someone, anyone vaguely suitable, to take over from Jacques Goddet and Félix Lévitan in the cockpit of the Tour de France. Goddet would soon turn eighty-two and was about to retire, while Lévitan had been fired over alleged book-keeping irregularities dating back to 1983 and his stillborn Tour of America project. Goddet had been the Tour's games master, its route designer and sporting conscience; Lévitan sat alongside him as the ruthless, often unpopular but eminently resourceful business brain. In tandem, they had directed every post-war Tour de France. Their successor would therefore face a monumental task – and the burden of two giant legacies.

Laughing wryly, Naquet-Radiguet says now that he was 'either the right man at the right time' or 'the wrong man at the wrong time'. Later, he reconsiders: 'No one wanted to direct the Tour after Lévitan and it took a poor idiot like me to say yes.' He isn't even sure whether he was interviewed: his chum at ASO had recommended him to the company founder and overlord, Philippe Amaury, and soon his feet were dangling under Lévitan's old desk.

For a man with next to no interest in professional cycling, directing the Tour could never be a voca-tion. But the timing and symbolism of the union did somehow feel right. 'I was coming back to France after a long time in Latin America, and what better way to do it than via the Tour de France?' Naquet-Radiguet asks now. In early interviews, he appalled the purists by pointedly referring to the Tour as 'a product' and, even worse, 'a brand'. At forty-four, *Le Monde* considered him a 'young wolf' – which he was compared to Lévitan and Goddet. The same newspaper put it to Naquet-Radiguet that he might do for the Tour what Mikhail Gorbachev was in the process of doing for the Soviet Union – implementing his own brand of perestroika ('re-structuring'). Naquet-Radiguet was tickled. 'I don't know whether Gorbachev will succeed in the Soviet Union, but I will definitely modernise the Tour!'

The Société du Tour and Goddet seemed at that point to have welcomed him. Goddet rechristened him Braquet-Radiguet, '*braquet*' being the French for 'gear'. Every time he used the moniker, the doyen of Tour bosses would let out a gravelly guffaw then give his new sidekick a friendly elbow in the ribs.

Starting the 1987 Tour in Berlin had been the old regime's idea. It seemed somehow apt and prophetic, though, that Naquet-Radiguet was taking his place alongside Goddet in the race director's car on such a landmark occasion. 'I don't want to turn the Tour into a circus,' Naquet-Radiguet had promised. But he was already rumoured to be plotting a *Grand Départ* in Tokyo, with the Japanese capital reportedly ready to stump up ten million dollars. There would soon be further speculation about a start in Quebec, Canada. And talk of London. Consequently, for all of Goddet's bonhomie and Naquet-Radiguet's self-deprecation, doubts about the latter's motives and credentials were bound to persist. Goddet never tired of reminding him, 'Well, Jean-François, in any case, you know nothing about cycling.' A self-proclaimed 'mafia' of French team managers made life even harder. 'They were the only ones who really didn't welcome me at all,' Naquet-Radiguet remembers. 'The riders, the journalists... they were fine. But the likes of [Système U manager] Cyrille Guimard tried to make my life very hard. Guimard was the most troublesome in the gang, let's say...'

Most of the riders barely saw or spoke to him. Stephen Roche, the race winner, has clear memories of a stocky, square-jawed, amiable-looking gentleman – his features accentuated by their juxtaposition with the tiny, increasingly frail Goddet. But the Irishman's recollections more or less end there, with a hazy mental picture of 'a nice guy who seemed to have come from nowhere, and whom no one knew'. The hundred or so accredited print journalists on that year's race (these days there are around 350) were more inquisitive and, initially at least, impressed. François Thomazeau, now a veteran of over twenty Tours, was reporting on the *Grande Boucle* for the second time in 1987. Thomazeau says there was 'a touch of the Jean Todt about Naquet-Radiguet' – presumably meaning that, like the Formula One mogul, he appeared as cut out for piano bars as he was for press conferences. 'But there was also a bit of the little Napoleon about him,' Thomazeau qualifies. 'He used to have his head out of the sunroof and he'd be waving at the crowds in the provinces, like a Roman emperor, a Nero. But he was actually a friendly, affable chap. I think he really professionalised the Tour.'

Officially, Naquet-Radiguet had decided and been told to treat his first Tour as work experience, a fact-finding mission. From the moment he arrived in May, though, he had been plotting and beginning to implement a radical makeover. 'I came into a completely archaic world, a completely dictatorial world. I say dictatorial because you'll know that Lévitan was the boss and he was a dictator. He had done magnificently to get the Tour to where it was, to build the brand, but as often happens with dictators, the people working under him weren't very happy. And it was totally, totally archaic.'

Thus, as he made his way around France, Naquet-Radiguet began taking notes. Not just on Goddet's modus operandi but on what needed to change. For example, the cloth banner over the finish-line and what he now describes as 'a podium that was some kind of pig tractor that we towed on the back of a lorry'. Both, he says, looked 'absolutely rubbish' on the TV pictures that he was now attempting to sell to the USA and Japan, among other far-flung 'markets' – another word that the old guard abhorred. He also wondered why existing and potential sponsors weren't being properly entertained. Stage starts seemed like the perfect place for hobnobbing but lacked any pomp or formality. Riders typically spent the hour before the *départ fictif* either perched on the boot or bonnet of their team-cars or chatting idly under parasols on a bistrot terrace. 'In a way it was nice because the riders were close to the people. They could sign autographs and chat with the punters. The Tour has lost some of that now,' says Thomazeau.

Roche echoes him: 'I think if cycling has survived all of the problems of the last twenty or thirty years, it's because of the human side of it. The fans feel drawn to the riders as people. Those old stage starts really used to encourage that. It's true that this has slowly been lost.'

In 1987, Naquet-Radiguet watched the riders loitering idly in side-streets and allowed the outline of his first and most enduring creation to take shape. He would call it the *Village Départ* and from 1988 it would fulfil the same role in the Tour as the Forum in Ancient Rome – a pre-stage melting pot for riders, sponsors, journalists, race officials and other *suiveurs*.

Nearly thirty years later, the present-day village
remains faithful to Naquet-Radiguet's vision: that of a
sprawling, open-air hospitality enclosure where sponsors can entertain guests or clients, be entertained, eat
and drink, and at least have the impression of min-
gling with some of the competitors. With the advent
of the team buses late in the 1990s, the traffic of riders in and out of the village has diminished slightly,
but the main reasons for their visits are still much the
same as they were in its first incarnation. As Roche
explains with a mischief-laced grin: 'You'd come to
look at the interesting stands, who was on the stand,
and what kind of welcome you got.'

In plainer English: the main attraction was girls.

After three weeks, Roche would ride onto the
Champs-Élysées in the yellow jersey, as the champion elect. He remembers drawing alongside the race
director's car to thank Jacques Goddet for everything
and wish him well in retirement. Sat beside Goddet,
Naquet-Radiguet wore a thin smile, not because he
resented the plaudits for his co-director, but because,
to him, ending the Tour with what amounted to a
procession, anti-climaxing in a bunch sprint, looked
like a terrible cop-out. He had already aired this view
to Goddet, only to be told, yet again, that he couldn't
tell an *echelon* from a *saucisson* and therefore wasn't
entitled to an opinion. Which perhaps he wasn't –
except that Naquet-Radiguet would soon be in charge,

with Goddet retaining just an advisory role. Naquet-Radiguet duly informed Goddet, his co-workers and underlings that, whether they approved or not, in future the Tour would finish with a time trial, to prolong suspense until the very last pedal stroke. If it couldn't be arranged for 1988, then this would definitely be the new formula from 1989.

In the media, he had already been praised as an innovator, by some even as a visionary. One of the most prominent Italian writers of the day, Gian Paolo Ormezzano, noted that, under Naquet-Radiguet's stewardship, the Tour was hurtling into a different dimension, commercially speaking, while the Giro and its devotees languished. In France they called it 'mondialisation'. 'Our riders arrive at the Tour and they're already sweating and out of their comfort zone, like peasants forced to wear dinner jackets,' Ormezzano wrote.

In the press-room, at least, most could acknowledge that the Tour had needed to start embracing change. The privatisation of French television had begun late in 1984 with the launch of Canal+. It continued through to 1987, when TF1 was deregulated. Suddenly, as a result, the Société du Tour could auction the rights to show the 1988 race to the highest bidder. This, at least, was how Naquet-Radiguet saw it. He negotiated a bumper new deal with TF1 in the hope that the current rights-holder, the state-owned Antenne 2, would match their offer. They didn't but still kept the contract for 1988 at Philippe Amaury's insistence. That year, TV revenue accounted for just 10 per cent of the Tour's total budget. Nowadays, it is well over half.

It was believed at the time that a fault line between Naquet-Radiguet and his employers had opened over the TF1-Antenne 2 conundrum. Nearly three decades on, Naquet-Radiguet says this is only partly true. He recalls that, after the 1987 Tour, as the months passed, he noticed resentment towards him growing among colleagues. In particular, he thought, they seemed jealous of his suave, relaxed manner in front of a camera and his fluency in foreign languages. 'I came from industry,' he says, 'and one of the things that I think shocked people was that I was pretty good on TV. That was part of my job. But I soon realised that there were some people who saw their image as their main priority and not just a way of boosting the Tour's earning potential. They thought that, if I was going on TV and it went well, I was stepping on their toes.'

His plan for the 1989 final-day time trial aside, he continued to leave sporting decisions to more qualified cohorts at the Société du Tour. Goddet still lurked in the background. And after his retirement in 1986, Bernard Hinault had been signed up as a technical advisor. Naquet-Radiguet says that he and the Badger got on famously. 'A lovely fellow,' is how Naquet-Radiguet describes Hinault now.

At the end of March 1988, Hinault and Naquet-Radiguet flew to Canada to continue talks about a *Grand Départ* from Quebec in 1992. That ill-fated project, though, would come to symbolise the Naquet-Radiguet era, which was now already drawing to a close. At the end of May, the Société du Tour announced that they and Naquet-Radiguet had parted company, almost a year to the day from his appointment. The 1988 race would be directed by the rather temporary-looking duo of Xavier Louy, a former politician who also happened to be Naquet-Radiguet's brother-in-law, and the *L'Équipe* boss, Jean-Paul Courcol. Hinault and Goddet would provide input on the sporting side.

It would be a disaster: a bland race on an insipid route, with a winner, Pedro Delgado, who had tested positive for a substance banned by the International Olympic Committee but not the UCI. Courcol would soon be returning to his full-time role at *L'Équipe*, while according to another newspaper, *L'Humanité*, Louy had been 'evicted'. When the 1989 route and the final-day time trial cooked up by Naquet-Radiguet was unveiled in October 1988, so too were two new chiefs: Jean-Marie Leblanc, who had done six Tours in Goddet's car as the Radio Tour announcer, would focus on the bikes, and Jean-Pierre Carenso on the business. In its coverage of the presentation, *L'Humanité* waxed lyrical about a route that 'buried Naquet-Radiguet's crazy extravagances'.

The relief at Leblanc's recruitment was palpable. He was one of the journalists' own, having written on cycling for *La Voix du Nord* and also *L'Équipe*. He was also a former rider. Asked to assess Naquet-Radiguet's contribution a month after his departure, Goddet had said tartly, 'Naquet-Radiguet had some qualities, he was a businessman, but he wasn't cut out for an active role on the race.' The old Cognac salesman's new position made him even easier to pooh-pooh: he had fallen straight into a job as commercial director of TF1, the company that he'd wanted as the Tour broadcaster.

* * *

What no one could take away from Naquet-Radiguet was his place on that illustrious list of Tour directors. Up to the end of the 1988 race, the roll of honour consisted of just five names: Desgrange, Goddet, Lévitan, Naquet-Radiguet and Courcol or Louy, depending on who you thought had really been steering the ship in 1988.

'In truth, there had been six directors up to that point,' says Philippe Sudres with a glint in his eye. We ask what he means. Sudres goes on to tell a story that had never previously made it into print, but is well known and the cause of enduring mirth among a few former employees of the Société du Tour.

Sudres thinks it was in Nancy at the end of stage eight of the 1988 Tour. The long-serving competitions director, Jean-François Pescheux, says it was Reims the day before. One of the race doctors at the time, Gérard Nicolet, tells us he agrees with Pescheux.

What they all remember is that, wherever it was, after one stage early in the 1988 Tour, a gentleman walked into the hotel where Société du Tour personnel were staying and told the receptionist that he was the new Tour de France director.

Nicolet recalls: 'I'm standing there at reception, waiting for my key to get into the room, when this guy shows up. 'I'm the next Tour director, so can you give me my room key?' The receptionist is just a young kid. He starts looking down his booking list, shakes his head, and tells the guy he doesn't have that name. The fellow leans forward and whispers to him, 'I'm here incognito. Just having a look, checking how it's all going, you know. What rooms do you have left…?' It was quite late, you see. Anyway, the receptionist takes another look at his list, is obviously panicking a bit, and finally says that France Inter or some other radio station haven't showed up, and that consequently there might be one room. And he gives the guy the key. I think, "Hmmm, OK." But I don't know. It was definitely possible that someone had been lined up as the new director. Admittedly, this chap didn't exactly look the type, in his baseball cap…'

Later that evening, Pescheux says, he arrived
in the dining room of the same hotel and was told
that the president of the Tour's regional committee
for Normandy was paying the race a surprise visit.
Pescheux was immediately confused: he knew the
president of the Normandy committee, and he wasn't
in the room. 'That's him, over there,' Pescheux was
told. But the face wasn't familiar. 'Anyway,' Pescheux
says, 'I went over and sat down next to this chap at
the table. "You're not the president of the Normandy
committee, are you?" I said to him. "Ah, no," he says.
"Vice-president. You don't know me because I don't
usually come to races." "*Ah, bon,*" I thought. It seemed
a bit odd, but then Jean-Pierre Courcol, the *L'Équipe*
director, sat down and started chatting to this guy. I
left them to it. For all I knew he could have been from
the Normandy committee…'

The next morning, Pescheux gathered up his
suitcase and went downstairs to find the mystery
guest waiting in the lobby. Goddet hobbled down
a few moments later. '*Cher* Jacques!' his purported
successor greeted him. On his way out of the front
door, Goddet then either offered or was persuaded to
give him a lift to the start. At the end of the short
journey, the two men then decanted from Goddet's
car at the entrance to the brand new *Village Départ*.
One of Goddet's Société du Tour colleagues saw them
and immediately provided the old director's new

friend with an accreditation. According to Gérard Nicolet, the gentleman then spent what remained of the morning reprising his routine from the previous evening to whomever asked and many who didn't. 'I'm the next director of the Tour. But shhhhhh! I'm here incognito.'

The secret couldn't last. Not the one about him being 'under cover' – which was a lie – but the one about his true identity. Nicolet, his fellow doctors, Gérard Porte and Alain Ducardonnet, Pescheux and Courcol held an impromptu meeting to compare stories. Nothing added up. It was decided that someone needed to intervene. Nicolet and Durcardonnet marched over.

'Alain was very calm,' Nicolet remembers. 'He said, "Look, *Monsieur*, there's a problem here. We're going to have to take care of you." To which the guy put a finger over his lips. Then he tells Alain, "Look, you know that I know that you know that I know that you know…" And went on and on like that. Alain said, "OK, but, *Monsieur*, we're going to have to do something with you…" And off he goes again: "I know that you know that I know that you know…" It was quite comical, but the guy was clearly a bit disturbed. Alain decided that we'd have to call an ambulance and get him taken away. He didn't put up any resistance. About two hours later, though, we got a call from the hospital: "You'll have to come and get this guy.

We can't do anything with him." But I said there was nothing that we could do, either. And I think that was the last we heard of it. The guy had been in some kind of institution or mental hospital, I think. He'd lost his wife and gone a bit batty or something. It was all quite sad.'

Pescheux agrees, while also confessing his admiration for such an audacious hoax. There are plenty of people who drift in and out of the Tour caravan under false pretences, he says, but usually with more modest aims. 'I can remember another time when I was at a hotel bar with a guy who claimed to be with the Peugeot team. He was buying drinks for everyone, telling the barman to put it on [team manager] Maurice de Muer's tab. Then at the end of the night he just put his glass down and left... There are so many people on the Tour that it creates confusion, and you can get away with stuff like that for a short while. But eventually people start to talk and say, "Who's that guy?" You can't sustain an act for long...'

* * *

Speak to Jean-François Naquet-Radiguet about conmen and tall tales nowadays and the seventy-four-year-old will smile knowingly. It was easy for uninformed commentators to dismiss him as a charlatan after he left the Société du Tour in 1987, but

history and a detailed examination of his achieve-
ments flatter Naquet-Radiguet and his brief reign.
'He was someone who really tried to freshen up the
Tour, and whose time on the race was really healthy
in my opinion. Naquet-Radiguet was there at a water-
shed moment for the Tour de France, and he was the
impulse behind a lot of things,' says Philippe Sudres.

Speaking to us from his Brittany home in August
2014, Naquet-Radiguet himself says that his memories of the Tour are almost exclusively sweet ones.
'OK, I met a bit of opposition, and there were a few
things that I didn't like.

'Overall, though, I don't think I've got anything to
be ashamed of, because, with hindsight, I think I got
things just about right. Now I regret that it didn't last
a bit longer but it was a fantastic adventure. I loved
the fact that being the Tour director opened so many
doors. For example, when I decided that we needed
to do something with the podium, show off the sponsors better, I called up the office of [legendary French
advertising magnate] Jean-Claude Decaux and got
passed straight to him.

'If you talk about legacy, there were a few things
that I did but only three that I really insist on being
recognised for: sorting out the podium, the *Village
Départ* and the time trial on the Champs-Élysées in
1989. Of course, you could say that Laurent Fignon
lost the Tour because of me. He lost by eight seconds.

I thought he was going to hunt me down and kill me! But that was the race! You either want sport, competition, a race, or you can have a procession. I thought we wanted sport.'

The tall tales, they would come later. Or the fables, to be precise. Yes, because, after his time at TF1 and another spell at a company manufacturing bar-code readers, Naquet-Radiguet discovered a new passion in retirement: he began writing fables – short stories with animals as the protagonists that invariably end with a moral or pithy conclusion. In a way it was ironic – he had been the first Tour director who wasn't also a published writer or journalist – yet he'd end up putting his name to several books. Well, not his name strictly speaking, but an intriguing *nom de plume*: Jean du Frout. The 'Frout' being a small brook that flows behind his house in Keremma, Brittany.

'I'd always loved writing, and I found that fables suited me perfectly,' he explains. 'I like writing that's succinct, lively, engaging, and I found that fables worked perfectly for that. I also wanted to make a show of my fables, not just write, so I have a pianist who performs them with me. We've done shows in Paris, Belgium, Cameroon, and I've done three books with a brilliant illustrator, Desclozeaux. We have a fourth on the way. I'm afraid there's absolutely no link to cycling in my fables! I still watch the Tour every now and then, but I keep the two things – my fables and my past life as the Tour director – completely separate.'

The musings of Jean du Frout contain lessons on grown-up themes like politics and relationships, but steer clear of sport. One fable entitled 'Oscar Pistorious at the Olympics' is a curious exception. More typical vignettes include 'The Dove and the Monkey', 'The Blue-Eyed Frog' and 'The Seven Coconuts'. 'I like to think the audience is pretty broad,' says their author. 'They've got the animals and the kind of narratives that might appeal to young kids, but then you've also got something like "The Oyster and the Lobster" which is all about class and ends with a socialist anthem!'

We point out that one animal seemingly lacking from his *oeuvre* is the badger or *blaireau*. He laughs – cycling's Badger, Hinault, is still his fondest acquaintance in the world of cycling. They caught up in 2013, when Naquet-Radiguet was invited by ASO to attend the centenary Tour. He chose the stage closest to home, the time trial to Mont St Michel. It was his first time at the *Grande Boucle* since that final day in 1987, when Stephen Roche shook Jacques Goddet's hand and told him farewell.

No one could have predicted at the time that Jean-François Naquet-Radiguet was also about to bid the Tour and cycling adieu. His brief time at the helm of the world's biggest bike race had been his destiny, and Naquet-Radiguet had believed in and honoured it.

His name and face faded from many memories long ago – much faster than his contribution will vanish from the Tour's present and future.

---

**Daniel Friebe** began writing on professional cycling midway through a modern languages degree at University College London in 2000. He has covered every Tour de France since 2011, when he was still comfortably qualified for the white jersey. Now *Procycling*'s European editor, he is the author of *Eddy Merckx: The Cannibal, Mountain High* and its sequel *Mountain Higher*, and collaborated with Mark Cavendish on his best-selling autobiographies, *Boy Racer* and *At Speed*. He is a co-host of the *Telegraph Cycling Podcast*.